JOIN IN

Developing Conversation Strategies

Student Book 2

Jack C. Richards
& Kerry O'Sullivan

OXFORD
UNIVERSITY PRESS

OXFORD
UNIVERSITY PRESS

198 Madison Avenue
New York, NY 10016 USA

Great Clarendon Street, Oxford OX2 6DP UK

Oxford University Press is a department of the University of Oxford.
It furthers the University's objective of excellence in research, scholarship,
and education by publishing worldwide in

Oxford   New York

Auckland   Cape Town   Dar es Salaam   Hong Kong   Karachi
Kuala Lumpur   Madrid   Melbourne   Mexico City   Nairobi
New Delhi   Shanghai   Taipei   Toronto

With offices in

Argentina   Austria   Brazil   Chile   Czech Republic   France   Greece
Guatemala   Hungary   Italy   Japan   Poland   Portugal   Singapore
South Korea   Switzerland   Thailand   Turkey   Ukraine   Vietnam

OXFORD and OXFORD ENGLISH are registered trademarks of
Oxford University Press

© Oxford University Press 2009

Database right Oxford University Press (maker)

Editorial Director: Laura Pearson
Executive Publishing Manager: Laura Le Dréan
Senior Managing Editor: Pat O'Neill
Director, ADP: Susan Sanguily
Design Manager: Stacy Merlin
Senior Designer: Michael Steinhofer
Cover Design: Michael Steinhofer
Image Editor: Fran Newman
Project Leader, ADP: Bridget McGoldrick
Manufacturing Manager: Shanta Persaud
Manufacturing Coordinator: Elizabeth Matsumoto

ISBN (STUDENT BOOK): 978 0 19 436776 9
ISBN (STUDENT BOOK WITH CD): 978 0 19 446055 2

Printed in China.

10 9 8 7 6 5 4 3 2 1

ACKNOWLEDGMENTS

Illustrations by: Adrian Barclay: 9, 26 (top), 75 (bottom); Barbara Bastian: 11, 17,
32 (bottom), 47, 68 (bottom); Ken Batelman: 23, 25, 74 (top), 77 (bottom); Grace
Chen: 53, 59 (bottom), 62 (top); Marcos Chin: 27, 39, 54; Kun-Sung Chung: 7,
45; Mona Daly/Mendola Art: 34, 61, 68 (top); Kevin Hopgood: 29, 33, 42, 57; Kim
Johnson/Lindgren & Smith: 10, 43, 73; Karen Minot: 26 (bottom), 32 (top), 35,
71; Marc Mones/AA Reps: 16, 19, 52; Christian Musselman: 20, 55, 76; Leif Peng:
13, 44; Jorge Santillan/Beehive Illustration: 12, 15, 37, 59 (top); Rob Schuster:
8, 50, 56, 62 (top); Kaylene Simmons/Lemonade Ilustration: 75 (top); William
Waitzman: 41, 50 (bottom), 63, 77 (top); Laurence Whiteley/NB Illustration: 6.

We would like to thank the following for their permission to reproduce photographs:

Cover: First row from left to right: Blend Images/Jupiter Images; Photo Alto/
Jupiter Images; Second row: Grapheast/Alamy: Jan Kassay; BrandX/Jupiter
Images; Bottom row: Dex Image/Jupiter Images; Taxi/DreamPictures/Getty
Images; Lushpix/Age FotoStock: (person holding a CD); istockphoto.com: (CD).

Interior: AGE Fotostock: Graziano Arici, 66 (Nureyev); Sylvain Grandadam,
67 (Miyake); Graziano Arici, 69 (Pavoritti); Interfoto, 71 (Picasso painting);
Elisabeth Coelfen, 72 (shoes); Alamy: Nicephoto, 6; Digital Vision, 14 (neck brace);
Blickwinkel, 14 (leg); Jupiterimages/Comstock, 14 (sling); D. Hurst, 18 (jeans); Siede
Preis/Photodisc, 18 (shirt); Nikreates, 18 (sandals); Photodisc, 18 (necktie); D. Hurst,
21 (belt); Emily Lai, 21 (bracelet); Kari Martitila, 21 (shorts); JupiterImages/Brand
X, 21 (socks); Imagebroker, 21 (boots); VStock, 30 (party); Foodfolio, 36 (candies);
Russells, 36 (flowers); Somos Images, 38; George and Monserrate Schwartz, 48
(camping); Ian Masterton, 49 (Taipei); Jim West, 49 (house); GoGo Images Corp., 51
(operator); ONOKY-Photononstop, 60 (cook); Jon Henshall, 60 (draw); INSADCO, 60
(photographer); Photos12, 66 (Charlie Chaplin); Photos12, 66 (Peter Jackson); V&A
Images, 70 (Beatles); Movie Magic, 71 (poster); D. Hurst, 72 (CD); Andrew Parterson,
72 (chocolates); Getty Images: Dorling Kindersley, 18 (scarf); Hugh Sitton, 24
(newsstand); Pinnacle Pictures, 30 (opened door); Olivia Barr, 31; John Giustina,
46; Fat Chance productions, 51 (guard); Stringer, 67 (band); Stringer, 67 (Yasunari);
WireImage, 69 (Blaine); WireImage, 69 (Kim); Jo Hale, 69 (Mae); Gareth Cattermole,
69 (Lam); MJ Kim, 71 (Lam); WireImage, 71 (Radcliffe); The Granger Collection:
66, 71; The Image Works: Bill Jones/Daily Herald Archive, 66 (Disney); Topham, 66
(Indira Gandhi); 67 (JK Rowling); Roget Viollett, 69 (Picasso); Topham/Keystone,
69 (JK Rowling); Inmagine: Comstock, 7 (saxophone); Stockbyte, 21 (tie, wallet);
Corbis, 22; Creatas, 30 (restaurant); Brand X, 36 (gift); Pixtal, 40; Glowimages, 48
(beach); Radius Image, 49 (lake); Digitalvision, 51 (bellhop); Bananastock, 51 (server,
receptionist); Digitalvision, 60 (tennis); Uppercut, 64; Photodisc, 72 (cap); Istock:
72 (t-shirt); Jupiterimages: Polka Dot Images, 28; Corbis, 51 (chef); Image100, 51
(driver); BlendImages/Kris, 56; Image Source Black, 58; Blend Images/Picturenet, 60
(piano); Blend Images/Andersen Ross; Radius Images, 76; Jupiterimages Unlimited:
Polka Dot, 60 (dancing); Mary Evans Picture Library: 60 (Mozart); Masterfile: Tom
Feiler, 18 (sneakers); Omni-Photo Communications: Anita Brause, 24 (convenience
store); David Parket, 24 (drug store); PhotoEdit, Inc: David Young-Wolff, 21 (sweater);
Bill Aron, 72 (magazine); Kayte M. Deioma, 51 (kitchen assistant); Punchstock:
Stockbyte, 7 (piano); Thinkstock, 14 (eye patch); Brand X Pictures, 14 (hand, foot);
Photodisc, 21 (necklace); Uppercut Images, 24 (supermarket); Bananastock, 47;
Uppercut, 48 (road trip); Photodisc, 51 (maid); Robertstock: Daniel Hurst, 21
(umbrella); Shutterstock: 18, Kristin Smith (slacks); Vasina Natalia: 18, (blouse);
Lepas: 21 (scarf); Ruzanna, 21 (earrings); Tony Sanchez-Espinosa, 72 (book).

The publisher would like to thank the following for their help in developing this series: Matt
Caldwell, Hannan University, Japan; Cheng-Chi Chan, School of Continuing
Education, Chinese Cultural University, Taiwan; William Davis, Daejin University,
Korea; Duane Dunston, UBest Language School/Chang-Shing Senior High School;
Taiwan; Janet M.D. Higgins, Okinawa University, Japan; Tom Harper, Taiwan;
Ward Ketcheson, Aomori University, Japan; Daniel T. Kirk, Yokkaichi University,
Japan; Kevin Lee, Kyung Hee University, Korea; Crystal Lin, Tzu Chi University,
Taiwan; Rick Romanko, Wayo Women's University, Japan; David Ruzicka, Shinshu
University, Japan; Stephen Shucart, Akita Prefectural University, Japan; Helen Song,
Sisa Language Institute, Korea; Keum Ok Song, BCM Language School, Korea; Ha
Jung Sung, Chungnam National University, Korea; Damien Tresize, Leader College
of Management, Tainan, Taiwan; Hajime Uematsu, Hirosaki University, Japan;
Tamami Wada, Nagoya Gakuin University, Japan; Ching-ping Wang, Tunghai
University, Taiwan; J. Scott Wigenton, Woosong University, Korea; Catherine Yang,
North Taiwan Institute of Technology; Rick Yang, Gram English School; Jeffrey
Lehman, LRD School; Soo Ha Yim, Hanyang University International Language
Institute, Korea.

Introduction

Welcome to *Join In*. This is a three-level speaking and listening series that teaches an important aspect of English: developing conversation strategies for *what* to say and also *how* to say it. This will help you improve your English.

Student Book

There are two lessons in each of the 12 units in the Student Book. Each lesson focuses on a different aspect of the unit topic. The lessons are organized into five sections, each one with carefully graded activities that provide opportunities to speak and listen.

Lesson 1

Lesson 1 begins with a conversation. It presents language and vocabulary that will be practiced throughout the lesson in context. **Language focus** presents and provides practice with a grammar point. The **Listen and Understand** activities help you to understand what people say. These sections help you improve your overall listening comprehension skills.

Lesson 2

Lesson 2 begins with presentation of more vocabulary related to the unit topic. **Conversation strategy** focuses on a feature of spoken English. This allows you to practice how to say what you want to say. Using these strategies will help you speak English in a more natural way. The **Listen and Understand** activities help you to understand what people say. These sections help you improve your overall listening comprehension skills.

Join in

Join in, the last section in each lesson, gives you the chance to speak to your classmates about the lesson topic. It also lets you practice the language focus and conversation strategy from earlier in the lesson.

Audio Program

There are various types of spoken English on the CDs—including casual conversations, telephone conversations, interviews, and messages. The complete audio program for the Student Book is on the Class CDs. There is also a Student CD on the inside back cover of this Student Book for self study. The Student CD contains the Conversations from page 1 of each unit (the conversation from Activity B and the practices from Activity C).

Scope and Sequence

1 CLASSROOM LANGUAGE

A. Use the expressions below to complete the conversations.

What's this called in English?   *What's a chef?*

What does "boring" mean?   *How do you pronounce this word?*

Could you repeat that?   *How do you spell that?*

1. **A:** _____

   B: Which word? This one?

   A: Uh-huh. That one.

   B: Comfortable.

2. **A:** _____

   B: It means not interesting.

3. **A:** _____

   B: A person who cooks food in a restaurant.

   A: _____

   B: C-h-e-f.

4. **A:** _____

   B: This? It's called a tennis racket.

   A: I'm sorry. _____

   B: Tennis racket.

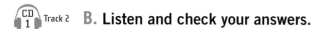 **B. Listen and check your answers.**

C. Pairs. Practice the dialogues above. Take turns.

2 SPELLING

A. Review the alphabet.

Aa	Bb	Cc	Dd	Ee	Ff	Gg
Hh	Ii	Jj	Kk	Ll	Mm	Nn
Oo	Pp	Qq	Rr	Ss	Tt	Uu
Vv	Ww	Xx	Yy	Zz		

CD 1 Track 3 **B. Listen and complete the missing information.**

First name: _____-U-Z-I-_____

Last name: _____-U-R-_____-H-Y

C. Pairs. Ask and answer these questions.

1. What's your name? How do you spell that?
2. Where do you live? How do you spell that?

Track 4 **A.** Listen and practice saying the months.

Months

January	July
February	August
March	September
April	October
May	November
June	December

 Track 5 **B.** Listen and complete the dates below.

	Name	Date
1.	Bob	January
2.	Sally	July
3.	Jun	February
4.	Alex	September

C. Pairs. Ask and answer these questions.

1. What date did English class start?
2. What is today's date?
3. What day is your birthday?

CD 1 Track 6 **A. Listen and practice saying the times.**

It's four o'clock.

It's ten after seven.

It's a quarter after eight.

It's half past six.

It's ten to two.

It's a quarter to nine.

B. Pairs. Look at these times. Say what time it is. Take turns.

1. **A:** What time is it?
   B: It's _____

3. **A:** What time is it?
   B: It's _____

2. **A:** What time is it?
   B: It's _____

4. **A:** What time is it?
   B: It's _____

CD 1 Track 7 **C. Listen and write times you hear.**

1. SQ21 from Tokyo _____
2. TG83 from San Francisco _____
3. SQ22 from Toronto _____
4. OM99 from Beijing _____

D. Pairs. Ask and answer these questions.

1. What time does English class start?
2. What time does class end?

1 WHAT KINDS OF MOVIES DO YOU LIKE?

A. Pairs. Check (✓) the kinds of movies you like. Talk with a partner and compare answers.

____ action ____ romance ____ horror ____ comedy ____ western

____ drama ____ animated ____ science fiction ____ musical

CD 1 Track 8 **B.** Listen to the conversation. Then practice with a partner.

A: Do you want to see a movie tonight?

B: 1 Maybe. What's on?

A: Well, there's a comedy with Eddie Murphy, I think.

B: No, I don't think so.

A: 2 Well, how about an action movie? There's a good Hong Kong action movie on right now. Do you like action movies?

B: Yes, I do. I like them a lot.

A: 3 Great. Let me check the Internet and see what time it's on.

C. Pairs. Practice the conversation again. Use this information.

Practice 1

1 Sure. What's showing?

2 Well, do you like Korean movies? There's one showing at the Rex.

3 OK. I'll pick up some tickets this afternoon.

Practice 2

1 OK. Are there any good ones at the moment?

2 Well, do you like musicals? I think there's one on this week.

3 Good. I'll check the movie times in the paper.

2 LANGUAGE FOCUS: QUESTIONS WITH *LIKE / INTERESTED IN*; OBJECT PRONOUNS

CD 1 Track 9   **A. Listen and practice.**

Do you like action movies?	Yeah, I like *them* a lot.
	Yes, I love *them*.
	They're OK.
	No, I don't like *them* very much.
	No, I can't stand *them*.
Do you like film music?	Yes, I really like it.
Are you interested in pop music?	Yes, I am. I like *it* a lot.
	No, I'm not very interested in *it*.
Are you interested in old movies?	No, I don't like *them* at all.

CD 1 Track 10   **B. Pairs. Complete the conversations with items from the language box in A. Listen and check your answers. Then practice with a partner.**

1. **A:** Do you like horror movies?
   B: Not really. I don't like _____ very much. Do you?
   A: Yes, I do. I like them a lot. One of my favorites is *Night of the Living Dead*.
   B: Oh, I never saw _____ .

2. **A:** Are you interested in action movies?
   B: Yes, I am. I always see _____ as soon as they come out.
   A: And what do you like about them?
   B: They're so exciting and fun. I really love _____.

3. **A:** Do you like classical music?
   B: No, not really. I find _____ a bit boring. What about you?
   A: Um, I really like _____.

4. **A:** Are you interested in jazz? Do you listen to _____ very much?
   B: No, I don't like _____ at all. How about you?
   A: I like some of the Japanese players.
   B: I haven't heard any of _____. Maybe I should check them out.

C. Pairs. Take turns asking and answering the questions above. Use true information.

3 LISTEN AND UNDERSTAND

A. Ted and Anna are talking about movies. Listen and check (✓) the kinds of movies they like.

	Horror	Sci-fi	Action	Comedies	Dramas	Not often	Pretty often
Ted							
Anna							

B. Listen again. How often do Ted and Anna go to the movies?

4 JOIN IN

A. What do you think about movies? Complete the survey for yourself.

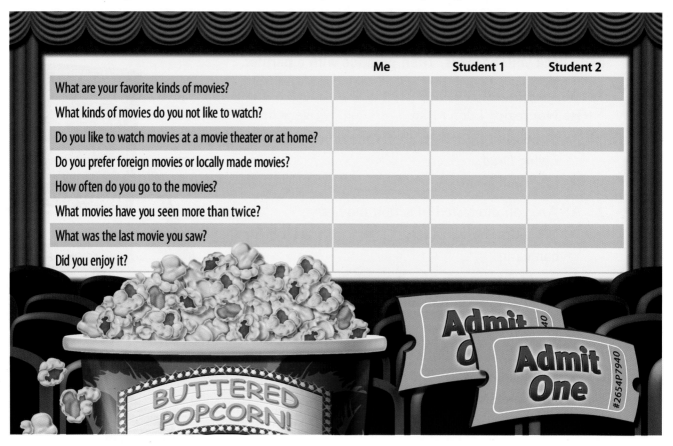

	Me	Student 1	Student 2
What are your favorite kinds of movies?			
What kinds of movies do you not like to watch?			
Do you like to watch movies at a movie theater or at home?			
Do you prefer foreign movies or locally made movies?			
How often do you go to the movies?			
What movies have you seen more than twice?			
What was the last movie you saw?			
Did you enjoy it?			

B. Groups. Ask and answer the questions from A with your group members. Ask and answer follow-up questions.

A: *Do you prefer to watch movies at a theater or at home?*

B: *I prefer to watch them at a movie theater.*

A: *Oh, do you have a favorite theater?*

A: *How often do you go to the movies?*

B: *I go about twice a month.*

A: *That sounds like fun. Who do you usually go with?*

1 THINGS TO DO AND SEE

CD 1 Track 12 **A.** Look at the events below. What do you think of them? Write your opinions in the chart below. Then listen and repeat.

1 = It sounds very interesting. **2** = It sounds OK to me. **3** = It sounds kind of boring.

a dance competition

a play

a talent show

a baseball game

a tae kwon do demonstration

a car show

an art exhibition

an ice-skating competition

a rock concert

B. Pairs. Ask and answer questions about the events. Are you interested in the same things?

A: What do you think about going to a dance competition?

B: It sounds very interesting. What do you think?

A: I agree. I think it sounds like fun!

C. Pairs. What are two things you would like to do this weekend? Talk with a partner.

A: I'd like to go to a concert. And I'd also like to see a movie. How about you?

B: I'd like to...

2 CONVERSATION STRATEGY: INVITING, ACCEPTING, AND DECLINING

🎧 CD 1 Track 13 **A. Pairs. Listen to the conversations. Then practice with a partner.**

1. **A:** *Would you like to do something on Saturday night?*

   B: *Maybe.* What are you thinking of?

   A: Well, there's a good movie showing downtown. It's a new action movie.

   B: *That sounds interesting.* What time is the first showing?

   A: It's at 8 o'clock. I can get tickets if you like.

   B: *Thanks. That would be great.*

2. **A:** *Do you want to go to the electronics fair on Saturday afternoon?*

   B: Saturday afternoon? *Oh, I can't. I have a guitar lesson in the afternoon.*

   A: Yeah? Well, how about on Sunday afternoon then?

   B: *Sure.* Sunday afternoon is OK for me.

   A: Great. Let's go to the exhibition after lunch.

   B: *OK. That's fine.*

B. Notice how we make invitations and respond to invitations. We can also use these expressions:

Inviting:	Accepting:	Declining and giving a reason:
Would you like to see a movie on Saturday?	*Sure. That sounds interesting.*	*Sorry, I can't. I have an appointment.*
How about seeing a movie on Saturday?	*Yeah. That would be great.*	*I'd like to, but I have a guitar lesson.*
Are you interested in seeing a movie on Saturday?	*Yes, a movie sounds fine.*	

Pairs. Now practice the conversations in A again, using different expressions to invite, accept, and decline.

C. Pairs. Use phrases from B to invite your partner to the events below. Your partner will accept or decline. Also add information of your own. Then change roles and practice again.

a car show on Friday night   a fashion show on Saturday afternoon

a pop concert on Saturday night   a picnic on Sunday afternoon

D. Pairs. Practice the conversations from A again. This time use your own information.

3 LISTEN AND UNDERSTAND

CD 1 Track 14 **A.** Listen to people talking about the events below. Write the dates and times for each event.

Event	Dates	Times	Tickets (adults)	Tickets (children)
talent show			$	$
film festival			$	$
ice-skating show			$	$

B. Listen again. Write the ticket prices in the chart above.

4 JOIN IN

A. This is your schedule for the week. Choose two evenings when you are busy and can't accept an invitation to go out with friends. Write the reason below.

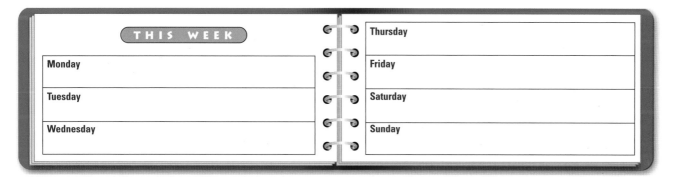

THIS WEEK

Monday

Tuesday

Wednesday

Thursday

Friday

Saturday

Sunday

B. Now write three events you would like to invite a classmate to do with you this week. Write the day and time also.

C. Groups. Invite classmates to the events you wrote in B. Check your schedule when you accept or decline an invitation.

A: Kazu, would you like to play video games on Thursday evening?
B: Sure, that sounds fun. What time...?

Health and Illness

LESSON 1: Health problems

1 WHAT HAPPENED?

A. What do you think happened to each person? Number the pictures below.

1. She broke her arm.   3. She fainted.
2. He twisted his ankle.   4. He got stung by a bee.

CD 1 Track 15 **B. Pairs. Listen to the conversation. Then practice with a partner.**

A: Wow! What happened?

B: 1 I broke my arm on Friday.

A: Oh, no! How did it happen?

B: 2 I fell off my bicycle going home from school.

A: That's too bad. Was it painful?

B: 3 Yes, it was pretty bad. Have you ever broken your arm?

A: No, I haven't, fortunately.

B: I don't recommend it!

C. Pairs. Practice the conversation again. Use this information.

Practice 1

1   I twisted my ankle over the weekend.

2   I was hiking in the mountains, and I just slipped.

3   Yes, it was. Have you ever twisted your ankle?

Practice 2

1   I broke my nose.

2   I ran into a glass door at work. I didn't see it at all.

3   Yes, it was. Have you ever done that?

CD 1 Track 16 **A. Listen and practice.**

Have you ever broken your arm?	Yes, I have.
	No, I haven't.
	Yes, I broke my arm a few years ago.
I've twisted	my ankle a couple of times.
He's also twisted	his ankle.
She's never twisted	her ankle.
I twisted	my ankle last summer.

CD 1 Track 17 **B. Pairs. Use the words in parentheses to complete the conversations. Use either the past tense or the present perfect. Listen and check your answers. Then practice with a partner.**

1. **A:** _____ you ever _____ (have) acupuncture?

   B: Yes, I _____ (have). I _____ (have) it many times.

   A: Why?

   B: I _____ (have) a lot of injuries from playing sports.

2. **A:** _____ you ever _____ (have) food poisoning?

   B: Yes, I _____ (have). I _____ (have) it about a year ago.

   A: What _____ (happen)?

   B: I _____ (eat) some bad seafood. I _____ (go) to the hospital.

3. **A:** _____ you ever _____ (be) in the hospital?

   B: Yes, I _____ (have). I _____ (be) in the hospital twice.

   A: Oh? Why _____ (be) you there?

   B: I _____ (break) my leg, and then I _____ (burn) my arm.

4. **A:** _____ you ever _____ (have) a bee sting?

   B: Yes, I _____ (have). I _____ (be) stung last summer.

   A: What _____ (happen)?

   B: We were camping when some bees _____ (sting) us.

C. Pairs. Practice the conversations again. Use true information.

A. Look at the pictures below. When do you use these items?

CD 1 Track 18 **B.** Listen to people talking about injuries. Number five of the pictures from 1 to 5 in the order you hear about them.

eye patch

neck brace

cast

bandaged arm

sling

bandaged foot

C. Listen again. What was each person doing when they got hurt? Number the events from 1 to 5 in the order you hear about them.

_____ going to work

_____ sunbathing

_____ cooking

_____ jogging

_____ playing sports

4 JOIN IN

A. Role play. It's been a terrible week. Everyone has a small injury. Practice conversations with different classmates.

A: *What happened to you?*

B: *I've got a sore neck.*

A: *Hmm. How did it happen?*

B: *I hurt it at the basketball game.*

A: *That's too bad. Is it painful?*

B: *Yes, it is.*

1 DRUGSTORE ITEMS

CD 1 Track 19 **A.** (Circle) the items you have used in the past month. Then listen and repeat.

1. cough drop

2. antacid tablets

3. aspirin

4. eye drops

5. bandage

6. antiseptic cream

7. muscle ointment

8. throat spray

9. lotion

B. Pairs. When do you use the items above? Talk with a partner. Use the words in the box.

A: What do you use muscle ointment for?
B: You use it for muscle pain. What do you use…?

C. Pairs. What else can you do for the problems in the box? Talk with a partner.

A: When I have a headache, I turn off the lights and try to relax.
B: That sounds like a good idea. Going for a walk usually helps my headaches go away.

➥ Try these

for a cut or scratch
for a cold
for an infection
for a sore throat
for muscle pain
for dry skin
for a sore eye
for a headache or fever
for indigestion

Track 20 **A.** **Pairs. Listen to the conversations. Then practice with a partner.**

1. **A:** Hi, Tim. How are things?
   B: Not too good. My throat's really sore.
   A: *That's too bad.* Have you taken anything for it?
   B: Not yet.
   A: You should get something from the drugstore.
   B: Yes, I will.

2. **A:** Hi. How are you feeling today?
   B: Much better, thanks. My throat is feeling much better today.
   A: *I'm glad to hear it.* What did you take for it?
   B: I got some medicine from the drugstore. It really worked well.
   A: That's good.

B. Notice how we can respond to news about someone's health. We can also use these expressions:

Responding to bad news: *That's too bad.*
     Sorry to hear that.
     Sorry you're not feeling well.

Responding to good news: *I'm glad to hear it.*
     That's good news.
     I'm glad you're feeling better.

Pairs. Now practice the conversations in A again, using different expressions to respond to bad and good news.

C. Class activity. Everyone in the class has been unwell or is just recovering from an illness. Ask several classmates how they are and give suitable responses.

A: Hi. How are you feeling today?
B: Terrible. I didn't sleep at all last night.
A: _____.

D. Pairs. Practice the conversations in A again. This time use your own information.

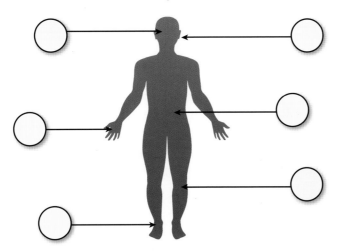

CD 1 Track 21 **A.** Listen to people describing health problems. Where is the problem? Number the body parts from 1 to 5 in the order you hear about them.

B. Listen again. What medicine does the doctor give the patient? More than one answer is possible. Check (✓) the correct answer.

	Drops	Antibiotics	Cream	Tablets
1.				
2.				
3.				
4.				
5.				

4 JOIN IN

A. Role-play. Take turns being a patient and a doctor at a health clinic. Use the sample dialogue and problems below. Student A looks at this page. Student B looks at page 78.

A: *What can I do for you today?*

B: *I have _____ .*

A: *That's too bad. How long have you had the problem?*

B: *For a week.*

A: *Mmm. I see. Well, I'll give you _____ .*

B: *Thank you very much.*

Problem	How long?	Treatment
a backache	a week	muscle cream and some tablets to take for the pain
an earache	three days	ear drops and some antibiotics

LESSON 1 : Describing preferences

1 WHAT KIND DO YOU PREFER?

A. Check (✓) the clothes you have bought in the past year.

| 1. jeans | 2. pants | 3. shirt | 4. top |

| 5. sneakers | 6. sandals | 7. scarf | 8. tie |

CD 1 Track 22 B. Pairs. Listen to the conversation. Then practice with a partner.

A: I'd like to get a couple of new shirts.

B: Something like the one you're wearing?

A: 1 No, something a little more stylish.

B: Well, have a look at these.

A: Yes, they look good. And I like the design. Are they silk?

B: Yes, they are. What do you think?

A: 2 Well, they're very nice, but I think I like these better.

B: They're cotton. Do you prefer cotton?

A: I do…

B: 3 And it's less expensive, too.

C. Pairs. Practice the conversation again. Use this information.

Practice 1

1   No, I prefer something more colorful.

2   They're OK, but I think these are nicer.

3   Yes, it's much cooler.

Practice 2

1   No, I want something more casual.

2   They're very nice, but these are much cheaper.

3   Yeah, and it's easier to wash too.

LANGUAGE FOCUS: COMPARATIVES

CD 1 Track 23   **A.** **Listen and practice.**

Which one do you *like better*?	I *like* this one *better*.
Which one is *more expensive*?	This one is *more expensive*.
Which ones are *cheaper*?	These are *cheaper*.
Which one costs *more*?	This one costs *more*.
Do you think this one is *good*?	No, I like this one *better*.
Silk is *more expensive than* cotton.	
It's *more comfortable*.	
Silk is *lighter than* cotton.	
Cotton is *easier* to wash.	

CD 1 Track 24   **B.** **Pairs. Use the words in parentheses to complete these conversations with comparatives. Listen and check your answers. Then practice with a partner.**

1. **A:** Which do you like _____ (*good*): dark colors or light colors?

   B: Light colors, I think. I think they suit me _____ (*good*).

   A: I do too.

2. **A:** Do you like cotton _____ (*good*) than silk shirts?

   B: Yes, I do. They're _____ (*easy*) to wash.

   A: Really? I like silk _____ (*good*).

3. **A:** Which do you think is _____ (*good*) for school: jeans or pants?

   B: Jeans, I think. They're _____ (*cool*) than pants.

   A: I agree. And they're _____ (*comfortable*) too.

4. **A:** Do you like to wear sneakers or shoes?

   B: I like sneakers better. They're _____ (*easy*) to clean.

   A: I like shoes better. I think they look _____ (*good*) than sneakers.

5. **A:** Do you think cotton socks are _____ (*warm*) than wool ones?

   B: No, I think wool socks are.

   A: I agree. And they feel _____ (*soft*) too.

C. **Pairs. Practice the conversations again. Use true information.**

3 LISTEN AND UNDERSTAND

A. Listen to people talking about the things below. Circle the one they prefer.

sunglasses   watches

jackets   shirts

sandals   shoes

B. Listen again. Why do they prefer each item? Check (✓) the correct column.
(More than one answer is possible.)

	Price	Quality	Brand	Color	Style
1.					
2.					
3.					
4.					
5.					
6.					

4 JOIN IN

A. Pairs. Which of these items of clothing are better for...the beach, school, the office, a job interview? Talk with a partner.

pants   shorts   a suit
a T-shirt   jeans   long-sleeved shirt

> I think pants are good for the office. They're more formal than jeans.

B. Pairs. Which clothes would you wear on these occasions? Why?
Talk with a partner.

a wedding   a barbecue   a long plane flight   a hike in the mountains

1 COOL THINGS

CD 1 Track 26 **A.** Look at the pictures below. (Circle) the things you are wearing today. Then listen and repeat.

1. earrings

2. belt

3. bracelet

4. shorts

5. socks

6. necklace

7. boots

8. umbrella

9. sweater

10. tie

11. scarf

12. wallet

B. Pairs. Which of the things from A do you have? Talk with a partner and compare answers.

I have a tie that's purple and gray.

You do? I don't have any ties.

C. Pairs. What do you think of the items above? Talk with a partner. Use the words in the box.

 Try these

stylish   attractive

old-fashioned   boring

cool

A. Pairs. Listen to the conversations. Then practice with a partner.

1. **A:** What's your favorite color for a shirt?
   B: I guess yellow. *I like bright colors.* What's yours?
   A: Mine is light blue. *I have lots of things that are light blue.*

2. **A:** Are you going shopping?
   B: Yes, I need to buy some shoes. *I want some for school.*
   A: Are you going downtown? Do you need anything else while you're there?
   B: Yeah, I really need some socks. *I haven't bought any for ages.*

3. **A:** Where do you like to go shopping?
   B: I like to shop at Superstore. *They always have good prices.* How about you?
   A: I usually shop at David Jones. *I like the staff there.*

B. Pairs. Notice how we often give additional information when we answer a question. Practice the conversations in A again, using different expressions to answer questions and give additional information.

C. Pairs. Think of extra information to add to these conversations. Then practice with a partner.

1. **A:** Have you bought any new clothes recently?
   B: Yeah, I bought some new boots last weekend. _____.
   A: Really?

2. **A:** Are you going shopping this weekend?
   B: Yes, I want to go to Superstore. _____.
   A: Yeah, it's a good place to shop.

3. **A:** Where did you buy that watch?
   B: I got it downtown. _____.
   A: It's really cute.
   B: Thanks.

4. **A:** Is that a new cell phone?
   B: Yes, it is. _____.
   A: Oh? Was it expensive?
   B: No, not really. _____.

D. Pairs. Practice the conversations in A again. This time use your own information.

CD 1 Track 28 **A.** Listen to people as they are shopping. Where do you think they are? Number five of the pictures from 1 to 5 in the order you hear about them.

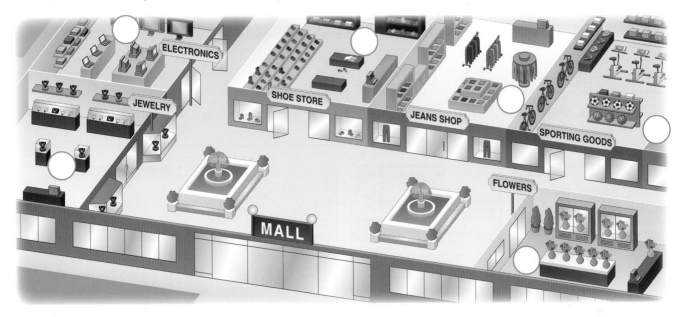

B. Listen again. Do they decide to buy something?

	Yes, they do	No, they don't
1.		
2.		
3.		
4.		
5.		

4 JOIN IN

A. Role-play. Take turns being a sales clerk and a customer in a clothing store. Use the information below and practice conversations like this.

A: Can I try on these shoes, please?

B: Sure. What size do you wear?

A: I usually wear size 9.

B: OK, just a minute please…here you are.

A: Thanks. Yes, these are good. I'll take them.

B: Sure. And how would you like to pay for them?

A: I'll use a credit card.

Item	Size	Payment
jeans	32	credit card
shirt	medium	cash
boots	10	check

4 The Neighborhood

LESSON 1: Neighborhood favorites

1 WHERE'S THE BEST PLACE TO SHOP?

A. Pairs. How often do you shop at these places? What do you usually buy there? Make some notes and then talk with a partner.

supermarket

newsstand

convenience store

drugstore

CD 1 Track 29 **B.** Pairs. Listen to the conversation. Then practice with a partner.

A: Excuse me. I'm new here. Can I ask you a few questions about the neighborhood?

B: Of course.

A: Great. 1 Well, first, where's the nearest supermarket?

B: There's one about 10 minutes from here, on Grey Street. It's pretty good.

A: Thanks. 2 And what about a bus stop? Where's the nearest one?

B: It's just around the corner.

A: Great. 3 Just one more thing. Where's the best place to walk my dog?

B: Oh, there's a nice park about 15 minutes north of here.

C. Pairs. Practice the conversation again. Use this information.

Practice 1

1 First, is there a good cafe around here?

2 And is there a post office in the neighborhood?

3 And also, where's a good place to jog?

Practice 2

1 First of all, is there a subway station nearby?

2 And how about a movie theater? Where's the closest one?

3 And what about a children's play area?

CD 1 Track 30 **A.** Listen and practice.

What's *the nearest* subway stop?	It's on Main Street.
Where's *the best* supermarket?	It's near the subway.
What's *the closest* park?	It's Brookdale, just around the corner.
What's *the busiest* street?	Main is *the busiest*.
Where are *the most interesting* shops?	In the mall.
Note: use *most* with *beautiful, famous, interesting, expensive, popular*	

CD 1 Track 31 **B.** Pairs. Use the superlative form of the words in parentheses to complete the conversations. Listen and check your answers. Then practice with a partner.

1. **A:** What's the _____ (*nice*)
      park in this neighborhood?
   B: Kennedy Park down by the river.

2. **A:** What's the _____
      (*interesting*) street for cafes?
   B: Oh, that's Ninth Avenue. It's a
      really cool place.

3. **A:** What's the _____ (*famous*)
      building in this area?
   B: The Science Museum.

4. **A:** What's the _____ (*close*)
      shopping mall?
   B: I guess it's City Central.

5. **A:** What's the _____ (*popular*)
      restaurant in the neighborhood?
   B: Oh, the Silver Moon. Everybody
      goes there.

6. **A:** Where's the _____ (*good*) place to jog or walk?
   B: Probably the college campus, I guess.

7. **A:** What's the _____ (*tall*) building in town?
   B: That apartment building on High Street, I think.

8. **A:** What would you say is the _____ (*busy*) street in the
      neighborhood?
   B: Oh, Market Street, for sure.

C. Pairs. Take turns asking and answering the questions above. Use true
information about your neighborhood.

3 LISTEN AND UNDERSTAND

CD 1 Track 32 **A.** Listen to Robyn talking about favorite places in her neighborhood. Number the places from 1 to 5 in the order you hear about them.

B. Listen again. What does she like most about each place?

	Friendly staff	Convenient location	Prices	Variety
1.				
2.				
3.				
4.				
5.				

4 JOIN IN

A. Answer these questions using true information.

What's a good place to hear live music? _____

What's the best fast-food restaurant? _____

What's the best place to hang out with friends? _____

What's the nicest place for a picnic or barbecue? _____

Where's a good place to go on a date? _____

Where's the cheapest place to buy interesting clothes? _____

B. Pairs. Ask and answer questions about preferences, using information you wrote in **A** and adding more information.

A: What's a good place to hear live music?

B: Joe's Cafe is good. They have a great jazz group there.

A: How often do they play?

B: Every weekend, I think.

1 NEIGHBORHOOD CONSIDERATIONS

CD 1 Track 33 **A.** Look at things people often think about when choosing a neighborhood. How important are they to you? Rank them from 1 (most important) to 9 (least important). Then listen and repeat.

safety and security

rents and costs

convenience

parking

noise levels

services

public transportation

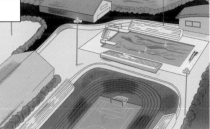

recreational facilities

schools

B. Pairs. Compare your answers from A. Do you agree on what's most important in a neighborhood? Talk with your partner.

A: *For me, convenience is the most important thing. I want to live close to the city.*

B: *For me, the most important thing is rents and costs. After that, the next most important is...*

C. Pairs. What else is important to you in choosing a neighborhood? Talk with a partner.

A. Pairs. Listen to the conversations. Then practice with a partner.

1. **A:** Hello. I'm in the apartment next door. *Sorry to bother you, but* your TV is very loud. *Would you mind turning it down?*

    B: *Sorry, I didn't realize* it was so loud. I'll turn it down now.

    A: Thanks a lot.

2. **A:** *Excuse me. Is that your* red car in the parking lot?

    B: Yes, that's mine.

    A: I can't get into my parking space. *Would you mind moving it, please?*

    B: *Oh, I'm sorry. I forgot* I parked it there. Let me go out and move it right now.

B. Notice how we can express complaints and apologies. We can also use these expressions:

Complaining:	Apologizing:
→ state the problem and request a solution	→ say you're sorry
I hate to bother you…	→ give an explanation
I hope it wouldn't be too much trouble…	→ offer to fix the problem
	I'm so sorry. I didn't remember…
	Why don't I… / Give me a minute and I'll…
	My apologies.

Pairs. Now practice the conversations in **A** again, using different expressions to express complaints and apologies.

C. Put the apologies in order.

1. [The neighbor's dog is barking.]

    A: Sorry to complain, but your dog is making a lot of noise.

    B: _____ I'll take him out right now.

    _____ Sorry, I didn't notice.

    _____ I guess he needs to go for a walk.

D. Pairs. Practice complaining and apologizing about the situations below.

1. You want your neighbor to turn down the radio. You're studying for an exam.

2. You want your neighbor not to play the guitar after 11 p.m. at night. You go to bed around that time.

3 LISTEN AND UNDERSTAND

CD 1 Track 35

A. People are complaining to the manager of their apartment building. Number the things they complain about from 1 to 5 in the order you hear about them.

	It has happened before	This was the first time
____ noise		
____ parking		
____ cleanliness		
____ elevator		
____ mail		

B. Listen again. Have these problems happened before? Check (✓) the correct column above.

4 JOIN IN

A. You are staying in a student dormitory. Think of complaints you have about the things below.

The issue	Your complaint
noise	
visitors	
the student lounge	
parties	
telephone calls	

B. Role-play. Think of a situation. One student is complaining. Another is responsible for the problem. Then think of another situation, switch roles, and role-play again.

A: Can I talk to you about the noise from your room?

B: What noise?

A: Sorry, but there's a lot of noise coming from your room at night.

B: Oh, sorry. My roommate and I love playing video games. We'll try to keep the noise down.

A: Thanks. That would be great.

1 HOW WAS YOUR WEEKEND?

A. Did you do any of these things last weekend? Circle the things you did.

| 1. eat out | 2. visit friends | 3. sleep in | 4. go to a party |

CD 1 Track 36 **B.** Pairs. Listen to the conversation. Then practice with a partner.

A: 1 So how was your weekend?

B: It was pretty good, thanks.

A: 2 Did you do anything interesting?

B: Well, I didn't do much on Saturday. 3 But on Sunday I went to a birthday party. It was fun. How about you? Did you have a good weekend?

A: 4 It was pretty good, thanks. I went to the swimming pool on Saturday.

B: Did you go with your girlfriend?

A: Yeah, I did.

C. Pairs. Practice the conversation again. Use this information.

Practice 1	**Practice 2**
1 Did you have a nice weekend?	1 Did you enjoy your weekend?
2 What did you do?	2 So how did you spend the weekend?
3 But on Sunday afternoon I went bowling.	3 But on Sunday I saw that new Jim Carrey movie.
4 I had a terrific weekend, thanks.	4 My weekend was pretty good, thanks.

2 LANGUAGE FOCUS: SIMPLE PAST QUESTIONS

CD 1 Track 37 **A. Listen and practice.**

Did you *have* a good weekend?	Yes, I did.
Did you *go* to a movie on Saturday night?	No, I didn't. I stayed home.
What *did* you *do* on Sunday?	I saw a movie.
Where *did* you *go*?	I went to a party.
Who *did* you *go* with?	I went with a few friends.
How *was* your weekend?	It was great.

CD 1 Track 38 **B. Pairs. Use the past tense of the words in parentheses to complete the conversations. Listen and check your answers. Then practice with a partner.**

1. **A:** _____ (*do*) you have a good weekend?

   B: Yes, it _____ (*be*) good, thanks.

   A: Did you stay home on Friday night?

   B: No, I didn't. I _____ (*see*) a concert at the college.

2. **A:** Where _____ (*do*) you go on Saturday night?

   B: I didn't go out. I _____ (*invite*) some friends over and we _____ (*watch*) a DVD.

   A: What movie did you _____ (*watch*)?

   B: We _____ (*see*) a Korean movie. It was a comedy. It _____ (*be*) funny.

3. **A:** How _____ (*be*) your Sunday? Did you go anywhere?

   B: Well, in the morning I stayed home. I _____ (*speak*) to friends online for a while. And then in the afternoon I _____ (*take*) my dog for a walk to the park. How about you?

   A: I _____ (*have*) a nice weekend. Some friends _____ (*come*) over and we played video games.

4. **A:** Did you study over the weekend?

   B: No, I didn't, actually. _____ (*do*) you?

   A: Yes, I _____ (*study*) all weekend.

   B: Wow. You didn't go out at all?

   A: Well, I _____ (*go*) for a walk on Sunday afternoon but that _____ (*be*) all.

C. Pairs. Based on the questions above, ask and answer questions about last weekend.

Track 39 **A. Listen to Roland talking about his weekend. Which of the things below did he do? Check (✓) the things he did.**

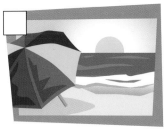
went to the beach

went to the mountains

watched a movie at a movie theater

went to the gym

caught some waves

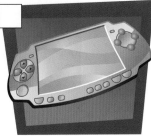
played video games

studied

went to a party

B. Listen again. Check (✓) which times Roland talked about.

____ Friday evening   ____ Saturday evening   ____ Sunday evening
____ Saturday morning   ____ Sunday morning
____ Saturday afternoon   ____ Sunday afternoon

A. Class activity. Talk to your classmates. Did anyone do the things below last weekend? Ask follow-up questions to find out more about what they did.

Did you meet anyone interesting?

Did you do anything unusual?

Find someone who...	Name
met someone interesting	
did something unusual	
bought a gift for someone	
bought something for themselves	
had a call from an old friend	
did something for the first time	
made an international call	
got home late one night	

B. Group activity. Share three interesting things your classmates did and answer any questions.

1 WEEKEND EVENTS IN TOWN

 Track 40 **A.** Have you ever been to any of these events? (Circle) the events you've been to. Then listen and repeat.

1. world music festival

2. farmer's market

3. dog show

4. speed car race

5. street festival

6. international food fair

B. Pairs. Which of the events in A would you like to go to? Which ones wouldn't you like to go to? Talk with a partner.

A: *Would you like to go to a world music festival?*

B: *Yes, I actually went to one in Hong Kong last summer.*

A: *Did you enjoy it?*

B: *Yes, it was fantastic. Would you...?*

C. Class activity. What interesting events are happening in your city this weekend? Talk to your classmates and see if they know about any interesting events.

A: *There's a fashion show at the Fashion Institute on Saturday afternoon.*

B: *Oh, yeah? I think there's a...*

2 CONVERSATION STRATEGY:
BUYING TIME BY ASKING DOUBLE QUESTIONS

CD 1 Track 41

A. Pairs. Listen to the conversations. Then practice with a partner.

1. **A:** Do you have any plans for the weekend? Are you going to watch the speed car race?

    B: I'm not sure. I haven't decided yet. *How about you? Are you going to watch the race? Do you like car races?*

    A: Definitely.

2. **A:** Do you like world music? Are you interested in going to the world music festival?

    B: Maybe. *But how about the street festival? Do you want to see what it's like?*

    A: Sure. That would be fun, too.

B. Notice that in conversation we often ask a general question first and then a more specific question. Practice the conversations in A again, using different questions to buy time.

C. Pairs. Add a suitable second question from the ones below to these conversations. Then practice with a partner.

> *Are you interested in seeing the new Nicole Kidman movie?*
> *Do you have any plans?*
> *Do you want to try some delicious Middle Eastern dishes?*
> *Do you want to check out the summer sales?*

1. **A:** Are you busy this weekend? _____

    B: I haven't made any plans yet. But there are a few things I need to do. Do you want to go to the mall? _____

    A: Maybe. I need to buy some running shoes.

2. **A:** Are you interested in going to the food fair on Saturday afternoon? _____

    B: Yeah. Why not.

    A: And how about on Saturday night? Do you want to see a movie? _____

    B: Sure. She's one of my favorite actresses.

D. Pairs. Practice the conversations in A again. This time use your own information.

3 LISTEN AND UNDERSTAND

A. People are calling a visitor information center for information about weekend events. Correct this information about the events.

Ice-Skating Competition

Saturday
Starts at 7:00
Main event at 9:00
National Sadium
Famous German ice-skater competing

Children's Singing Competition

Saturday evening
Skate championship
Tickets: $9 (children free)
Golden Park

International Food Festival

Tomorrow
Entry fee
Starts at 5:00
King's Cross

B. Listen again. Do you think the caller is likely to attend each event? Circle the main reason for their decision.

	Yes	No	Main reason		
1.			the cost	the location	the competitors
2.			the cost	the location	the timing
3.			the cost	the location	the date

4 JOIN IN

A. Class activity. Talk to four classmates and find out what their weekend plans are. Complete the chart.

Name	Weekend plans

B. Group activity. Talk about what you found out in A.

Is anybody you spoke to...

> *doing anything that sounds like fun?*
>
> *going somewhere exciting?*
>
> *planning to do something unusual?*

A: Tony's doing something that sounds like fun. He's going to enter a talent show on Friday night.

B: I hope he wins a prize.

LESSON 1: Things to remember

1 WHAT CAN I BRING?

A. What do you usually take when a friend invites you to their house for supper? Check (✓) the things you usually take.

____ candies ____ flowers ____ a small gift ____ something else ____ nothing

CD 1 Track 43 **B. Pairs. Listen to the conversation. Then practice with a partner.**

A: My American friend has invited some of us to her house on Saturday.

B: That's nice. Is it a dinner party?

A: Yes, it is. **1** Do you think I need to bring anything?

B: Well, yes, maybe you could take some flowers or some chocolates. **2** But you don't need to bring any food.

A: OK. And she said to come at around 7 o'clock. **3** So, does that mean exactly at 7 o'clock?

B: No, it's all right to come a little later, say at 7:15, but not earlier.

C. Pairs. Practice the conversation again. Use this information.

Practice 1

1 Do you think I ought to bring something?

2 But you shouldn't spend more than about $10.

3 So, should I arrive right on time?

Practice 2

1 What's the custom? Do I have to bring anything?

2 But you don't have to spend more than a few dollars.

3 So, do people usually arrive on time?

D. Groups. Talk to several classmates to find out who arrives on time to a party, and who comes late. Ask follow-up questions to learn more.

2 LANGUAGE FOCUS: VERBS OF OBLIGATION

A. Listen and practice.

What do I *have to* bring?	You *don't have to* bring anything.
What *should* he bring?	He *has to* bring a gift.
Do we *have to* bring anything?	You *could* bring some flowers.
Does she *need to* bring something?	She *ought to* bring something.
You *shouldn't* arrive late.	
You *need to* arrive on time.	

B. Pairs. Complete the conversation with items from the language box in A and the words below. Listen and check your answers. Then practice with a partner.

A: I've been invited to my teacher's house for dinner. What kind of clothes _____ I wear?

B: Well, you _____ wear anything too formal. You should try to dress "smart casual."

A: OK. And what time _____ I arrive? Is it OK to get there early?

B: No, you _____ arrive early. It's all right to arrive a little late, but you shouldn't arrive too late. You _____ to be there about 10 or 15 minutes after the time your host has said.

A: And what about bringing a friend? Is it OK to bring a friend?

B: No, you _____ bring a friend unless you ask your host first.

A: And do I _____ to bring anything, like a gift or something?

B: Well, you _____ bring something if you like, maybe some flowers.

Try these

ought	shouldn't
could	have
should	need

C. Pairs. Make a list of things to bring on the occasions listed below. Talk about them with a partner.

a child's birthday party

your grandparents' wedding anniversary dinner

a school picnic

a friend's high school graduation

A: What do you think you should bring for a child's birthday party?

B: Oh, I guess you ought to bring a gift...

A: Yeah, or maybe you could bring...

A. Sami is going to a bridal shower. Listen and circle the advice her friends give her.

1. You *should / shouldn't* bring a gift.
2. Guests *can / shouldn't* buy something together.
3. You *should / shouldn't* bring some food to the party.
4. Guests *need to / shouldn't* arrive exactly on time.
5. You *need to / don't need to* call if you want to bring a friend.
6. You *should / shouldn't* invite male friends.

B. Listen again and select the best option based on the advice.

1. food to bring	**a.** nothing	**b.** spring rolls	**c.** steak
2. gift to bring	**a.** a CD	**b.** a book	**c.** a vase
3. time to arrive	**a.** 2:00	**b.** 2:15	**c.** 3:00
4. what to wear	**a.** jeans and a T-shirt	**b.** a suit and hat	**c.** slacks and blouse

4 JOIN IN

A. Pairs. What does a visitor to your country need to know about the following customs in your country? Work with a partner and give suggestions for each situation.

Situation	Things it is good to do	Things to avoid
When you visit someone at their house		
When you meet someone for the first time		
When you eat at a restaurant with friends		

B. Groups. Compare your answers from A with your group.

A: *When you visit someone's house, you need to let them know you're coming. You shouldn't just drop in on them.*

B: *Right. And you ought to…*

1 LOCAL CUSTOMS

CD 1 Track 47 **A.** Match each custom with a situation when it usually happens (answers can be used more than once). Then listen and repeat.

1. on someone's birthday
2. on a national holiday
3. on someone's wedding day
4. at a special time of the year
5. on an anniversary day
6. at New Year's

sing traditional songs

send a card

give money

wear special clothes

eat special food

exchange gifts

light firecrackers

give flowers

put up decorations

B. Pairs. Are there other times in your country when you do any of the things from A? Talk with a partner.

A: *We can send a card when someone is sick.*

B: *Yeah, and also…*

C. Pairs. What customs do you have that aren't listed in A? Talk with a partner.

> People sometimes light firecrackers on a national holiday.

Track 48 **A.** **Pairs. Listen to the conversations. Then practice with a partner.**

1. **A:** We often give people flowers on their birthday.

    B: *So does that mean* you give flowers to men as well as women?

    A: Well, we usually give flowers just to women.

2. **A:** We normally sing traditional songs for family celebrations.

    B: *So you don't* sing them at other times of the year?

    A: Yes, we do sometimes.

3. **A:** We don't normally bring anything when we're invited to someone's house for a meal.

    B: *So that means* I don't need to buy something like flowers or chocolates?

    A: That's right. People don't expect anything.

B. **Notice how we can clarify our understanding of what people say. We can also use these expressions:**

So are you saying...   *Do you mean that...*   *Oh, does that mean you can...*

Pairs. Now practice the conversations in A again, using different expressions to clarify understanding.

C. **Pairs. Choose expressions to clarify understanding in these conversations. Then practice with your partner.**

So does that mean you'll be buying some tomorrow then?

So does that mean you don't give her a gift?

So you don't put them up at other times of the year?

1. **A:** We usually cook breakfast for our mom on Mother's Day.

    B: _____

    A: Oh, no. We do that, too.

2. **A:** We always put up decorations in the house on a national holiday.

    B: _____

    A: No. We put them up at other times, too.

3. **A:** We usually buy flowers for our children's teacher on the first day of school.

    B: _____

    A: Yes, I guess we should.

D. **Pairs. Practice the conversations in A again. This time use your own information.**

3 LISTEN AND UNDERSTAND

CD 1 Track 49 **A.** **Listen to people talking about customs. Number the pictures from 1 to 5 in the order you hear about them.**

taking shoes off

bringing a birthday cake

bringing gifts to a wedding

writing a thank-you note

giving gifts at a baby shower

throwing confetti at a wedding

B. **Listen again. Check (✓) the statements that are true.**

1. People in Matthew's country don't usually take their shoes off before entering a house. _____

2. They both have similar customs regarding birthdays. _____

3. James gave advice about how much the gift should cost. _____

4. Malee is planning to call her professor. _____

5. People sometimes bring food to this type of party. _____

4 JOIN IN

A. **Pairs. Imagine you are on a school visit to another country. You have to give a short presentation to a school group on some customs in your country. Work with a partner and prepare a short talk on how you normally celebrate these events.**

an important birthday   a wedding anniversary
a high school graduation   the birth of a new baby

B. **Group activity. Take turns making your presentation from A to others. They may want to ask for clarification, so be ready to answer questions.**

> We'd like to start by telling you how we celebrate an important birthday. In our country the child's first birthday is an important event. We usually…

unit
7 Stories and Explanations

LESSON 1: Cause and effect

1 **TELL ME ABOUT IT!**

A. Pairs. Look at these pictures. Talk with your partner about what you think happened in each case.

CD 2 Track 2 · **B.** Pairs. Listen to the conversation. Then practice with a partner.

A: Hey. What happened to your car?

B: **1** Oh, I ran into a wall while I was parking it the other day.

A: Oh, that's too bad. How did you do that?

B: **2** Oh, you know, I was talking on my cell phone, and I wasn't paying attention.

A: Well, I guess your insurance won't pay for that if it was your fault.

B: **3** No, they won't.

C. Pairs. Practice the conversation again. Use this information.

Practice 1

1 I had a little accident while I was driving the other day.

2 I bumped into another car while I was passing it, and I scratched it.

3 I guess not.

Practice 2

1 I damaged it while I was taking it out of the garage last night.

2 I was parked too close to the wall, and I wasn't looking where I was going.

3 I don't suppose so, but it's worth a try.

D. Pairs. Close your books and practice the conversation again. Use your own words.

2 LANGUAGE FOCUS: PAST TENSE AND PAST CONTINUOUS

 Track 3 **A. Listen and practice.**

I *ran* into a wall	while I *was parking* the car.
I *damaged* the car	while I *was taking* it out of the garage.
I *bumped* into another car	while I *was passing* it.

Track 4 **B. Pairs. Use the words in parentheses to complete the conversations. Use the past tense or the past continuous. Listen and check your answers. Then practice with a partner.**

1. **A:** How did you break your glasses?
   B: I _____ (*drop*) them while I _____ (*get*) out of a taxi.
   A: Oh, no. That's a shame.

2. **A:** How did you lose your wallet?
   B: It _____ (*fall*) out of my pocket when I _____ (*jog*) in the park.
   A: Yeah, that happened to me once.

3. **A:** What happened to your leg?
   B: I _____ (*break*) it while I _____ (*play*) ice hockey.
   A: Oh, that sounds painful.

4. **A:** How did you damage your watch?
   B: I _____ (*drop*) it when I _____ (*show*) it to my friend.
   A: Oh, that's too bad.

5. **A:** How did you damage your bike?
   B: I _____ (*hit*) another bike when I _____ (*ride*) to school.
   A: That's going to be expensive to fix.

6. **A:** How did your scratch your face?
   B: I _____ (*play*) with my dog in the park when she _____ (*scratch*) me.
   A: Oh, I see. I'm sure she didn't mean to do it.

C. Pairs. Practice the conversations in B again. Suggest other explanations for each of the problems.

A: How did you break your glasses?
B: I left them on the chair, and my brother sat on them.
A: No way!

3 LISTEN AND UNDERSTAND

A. Listen to people explaining how these things happened. Number five of the things they talk about from 1 to 5 in the order you hear about them.

B. Listen again. What was each person doing when it happened? Choose from the answers below.

1. _____   **a.** riding   4. _____   **d.** talking

2. _____   **b.** throwing   5. _____   **e.** cooking

3. _____   **c.** running

4 JOIN IN

A. Pairs. Great excuses! Take turns thinking of creative explanations for the following situations.

1. You borrowed your friend's bicycle and got a scratch on it.

2. You borrowed your friend's book and got coffee stains on it.

3. You borrowed a DVD and damaged it.

4. You borrowed your brother's digital camera and lost it.

5. You borrowed a white T-shirt and returned it with a tear in it.

6. You arrived home from school without your shoes.

> Oh, dear. What happened? My bicycle has a scratch on it.

> I know. I'm so sorry. But it wasn't my fault. This is what happened...

LESSON 2: Problem situations

1 UNFORTUNATE EXPERIENCES

 Track 6

A. Look at these problems. Check (✓) the things that have happened to you. Then listen and repeat.

1. You lost your cell phone.

2. You got robbed.

3. You missed an important appointment.

4. You lost your ID.

5. You forgot your best friend's birthday.

6. You got lost in a city.

7. You borrowed something from a friend and damaged it.

8. An airline lost your suitcase.

9. You tripped and fell.

B. Groups. Talk about the problems in A with your group. Ask and answer questions to find out what happened.

> Have you ever lost your cell phone?

C. Pairs. Have you experienced any other difficult situations like the ones above? Talk with a partner.

> Yes, I lost it last month.

Track 7

A. **Pairs. Listen to the conversation. Then practice with a partner.**

A: Have you ever lost your wallet?

B: Yes, I lost my wallet once when I was on vacation.

A: Really. *What happened?*

B: I took a taxi to visit a friend, and when I got there my wallet was missing. I think I dropped it while I was getting into the taxi.

A: *So what did you do?*

B: Well, I asked the driver to go back to where I got into the taxi.

A: *So then what happened?*

B: Luckily it was still there on the side of the road.

B. **Notice how we can keep a story going by asking follow-up questions. We can also use these expressions.**

How did that happen?   *What did you do after that?*

So what happened next?   *Did you ever find it?*

Pairs. Now practice the conversations in A again, using different expressions to keep the story going.

C. **Pairs. Put these sentences in the correct order to tell a story. Then take turns telling the stories and asking follow-up questions like the ones above.**

1. ____ I cancelled my credit cards and asked my parents to send more money.

   ____ I was visiting a crowded museum.

   ____ I got pickpocketed last year in Italy.

   ____ When I came out, my wallet was gone.

2. ____ Someone left it at the front desk for me.

   ____ I left it on a table in the library.

   ____ I went back to look for it, but it wasn't there.

   ____ I lost my wallet last month.

3. ____ I got into trouble with my best friend last week.

   ____ I bought her a more expensive new one.

   ____ I borrowed her cell phone and then lost it.

   ____ She forgave me.

D. **Pairs. Practice the conversation in A again. This time use your own information.**

CD 2 Track 8

A. Listen to the story and number the events in the correct order.

____ her brother came home

____ she put the washing machine on

____ she watched TV

____ she discovered the problem

B. Listen again. Check (✓) if these statements are True (T) or False (F).

	True	False
1. She washed her clothes at the hospital.	☐	☐
2. Her kid brother helped her with the washing.	☐	☐
3. She made a mistake when she put the clothes in the machine.	☐	☐
4. She watched television while the machine was on.	☐	☐
5. She wanted to change the color of her uniform.	☐	☐

4 JOIN IN

A. Pairs. Practice conversations about the story below. Ask follow-up questions to keep the story going.

One of you got lost on vacation in Seoul last summer. You went out for a walk and got lost. You didn't have any money with you. You asked a few people for directions, but they couldn't help you. You called the hotel to ask for directions. They told you how to get back to the hotel.

A: So, where were you going when you got lost?

B: I was trying to find a restaurant, but …

1 WHERE ARE YOU GOING TO GO?

A. What kind of summer vacation would you prefer? Rank these ideas from 1 (most interesting) to 5 (least interesting).

____ a vacation at a local beach   ____ staying home and doing nothing

____ a camping trip in the mountains   ____ a long car trip with your family

____ a visit to a foreign country

CD 2 Track 9   **B.** Pairs. Listen to the conversation. Then practice with a partner.

A: 1 What are you going to do for summer vacation?

B: I'm going to go to Indonesia.

A: Indonesia? That sounds interesting. Where will you go while you're there?

B: I'll be going to Java and Bali.

A: Bali. Wow. I hear it's fantastic. 2 And will you go with a group?

B: No, I'm going to go on my own. 3 But I'll meet up with a friend there and we'll travel around together.

A: So how long will you be there?

B: 4 I'll be there for about a month.

C. Practice the conversation again. Use this information.

Practice 1	Practice 2
1 What are your plans for the summer?	1 Have you made any plans for the summer?
2 Will you go with friends?	2 Are you going to go with your family?
3 But a friend is joining me there.	3 I like traveling by myself.
4 For a few weeks.	4 I'll be there for over a month.

2 LANGUAGE FOCUS: *GOING TO* AND *WILL* FOR FUTURE

CD 2 Track 10 **A. Listen and practice.**

What are you *going to* do for summer vacation?	I'*m going to* go to Indonesia.
What *will* you *do* for summer vacation?	I'*ll* probably *go to* Indonesia.
Are you *going to* travel with friends?	Yes, I *am*.
Will you travel with friends?	Yes, I *will*. / No, I *won't*. No, I'*m* not *going to*.

CD 2 Track 11 **B. Pairs. Complete the conversations with items from the language box in A. Listen and check your answers. Then practice with a partner.**

1. **A:** Where are you _____ to go for your next vacation?
   B: I'm _____ to go hiking with some friends.
   A: Oh, yeah? Where _____ you go?
   B: We'll probably take the train to the lake and hike in the mountains behind the lake.
   A: That _____ be terrific.

2. **A:** _____ you going to do anything for the long weekend?
   B: Not really. How about you?
   A: Yes, _____ going to visit some friends at the shore.
   B: That'll be nice. What are you _____ to do there?
   A: Oh, I guess we'll just relax and enjoy the ocean.

3. **A:** _____ you be here for the summer?
   B: No, I'm going _____ go to Taiwan.
   A: Yeah? What _____ you going to do there?
   B: I'm going to take a Chinese course in Taipei.
   A: Good luck. How long _____ you be there?
   B: _____ be there for six weeks altogether.

C. Pairs. Take turns asking and answering the questions above. Use true information.

3 LISTEN AND UNDERSTAND

A. People are talking about their vacation plans. Listen and check (✓) the chart. More than one answer is possible.

Who is going to...	Jun-hao	Carla	Martin	Anna
help make something?				
take a train trip?				
use her computer skills?				
just relax at home?				

B. Listen again. Check (✓) if these statements are True or False.

	True	False
1. Jun-hao doesn't have a lot of money this year.	☐	☐
2. Carla is going to work to help pay for her trip.	☐	☐
3. Martin and his uncle will work with a team of people.	☐	☐
4. Anna applied to work on the film.	☐	☐

4 JOIN IN

A. Pairs. Interview a partner about their vacation preferences. Check (✓) their answers. Ask follow-up questions to get more information.

1. What kind of places do you prefer?
   ____ big cities   ____ small towns
   ____ the mountains

2. Who do you like to travel with?
   ____ a group   ____ one other person
   ____ nobody

3. What do you like to do on vacation?
   ____ shop and go sightseeing   ____ meet new people
   ____ just relax

4. Where do you prefer to stay?
   ____ at a hotel   ____ at a youth hostel
   ____ with friends or family

B. Pairs. Suggest a good vacation for your partner based on the information you learned in A.

Well, you like big cities, you like to travel with a group, and...so I think you should...

1 HOTEL JOBS

CD 2 Track 13 **A.** In which jobs do you do these things? Number the pictures below (more than one answer is possible). Then listen and repeat.

1. wear a uniform **3.** work outside **5.** talk to guests
2. work in an office **4.** work in a restaurant

bellhop

telephone operator

security guard

chef

server

receptionist

room attendant

driver

kitchen assistant

B. Pairs. Do you know anyone who has one of the jobs from A? Talk with a partner.

A: A friend of mine is a chef. She works at the Shang Hotel.
B: How does she like it there?
A: Oh, she likes it a lot.

C. Pairs. What other jobs can people do in a hotel? Talk with a partner and make a list. Then compare lists with another pair.

2 CONVERSATION STRATEGY: USING QUESTIONS TO CONFIRM UNDERSTANDING

Track 14 **A.** **Pairs. Listen to the conversations. Then practice with a partner.**

1. **A:** How was your vacation?
   B: It was great, thanks.
   A: *The flights were good?*
   B: Yes, they were.

2. **A:** How was the hotel restaurant?
   B: It was so-so.
   A: *The food wasn't very good?*
   B: No, and the meals were expensive.

B. **Notice how we sometimes respond to comments with sentences that have rising intonation. We use these to confirm our understanding. We can also use these expressions:**

You had a good time?

You were able to relax and enjoy yourself?

The service was bad?

You didn't like your food?

Practice the conversations in A again, using different expressions to confirm understanding.

C. **Pairs. Add confirming questions from the ones below to these conversations. Then practice with a partner.**

You took tourists around sightseeing?

You worked in a restaurant?

You wore a uniform?

You want to earn extra money?

1. **A:** I got a part-time job last summer as a kitchen assistant.
   B: _____
   A: Yes, in that hotel down by the beach.

2. **A:** Every summer my classmates and I work at the Metro Hotel.
   B: _____
   A: No, it's part of our training. We work as receptionists.

3. **A:** Last summer I got a job as a driver at that new hotel downtown.
   B: _____
   A: No, just to and from the airport.

4. **A:** I worked as a security guard last summer.
   B: _____
   A: Yes, it was really cool. Dark blue and white.

D. **Pairs. Practice the conversations in A again. This time use your own information.**

3 LISTEN AND UNDERSTAND

 Track 15 **A.** Listen to people talking about vacation experiences. Check (✓) what they liked about the experience. Write X about what they did not like.

		Flight	Hotel	Tours	Food	Surprised	Not surprised
1.	Pei-ting						
2.	Miguel						
3.	Lilly						
4.	Kazu						

B. Listen again. Were their friends surprised? Check (✓) the correct column above.

4 JOIN IN

A. Pairs. Complete this survey about your last vacation. Then compare with a partner. Ask follow-up questions to find out more information.

QUESTION	ANSWER
Where did you go?	
Who did you go with?	
How long were you there?	
Where did you stay?	
What did you do there?	
How was the food?	
Did you buy anything there?	
What did you like most about it?	

A: *Where did you go on vacation?*

B: *I went to... What about you? Where did you go?*

A: *I went to...*

B. Pairs. Work together to make up your dream vacation. Then answer the questions from A about this dream vacation.

1 DO YOU WATCH MUCH TV?

A. Check (✓) your favorite free-time activities. Talk with a partner and compare answers.

1. watching TV

2. reading

3. playing sports

4. listening to music

CD 2 Track 16 **B.** Pairs. Listen to the conversation. Then practice with a partner.

A: So, do you watch much TV?

B: **1** I guess so. I usually watch it in the evenings before I go to bed.

A: What kind of programs do you like to watch?

B: **2** Oh, you know. The usual. Soap operas, movies, and sports.

A: **3** I watch a lot of documentaries. I love the National Geographic channel.

B: Yeah, it's great, isn't it?

A: It is. **4** I really enjoy nature programs.

B: Do you? I don't watch them much myself.

C. Pairs. Practice the conversation again. Use this information.

Practice 1

1 Yes, I watch it a lot.

2 Mostly news and documentaries.

3 I like documentaries too.

4 I also enjoy watching old movies.

Practice 2

1 Sure. I love TV.

2 Oh, I just watch whatever is on.

3 I have a few favorite programs.

4 I also love game shows.

D. Do you watch a lot of TV? Practice the conversation again. Use your own ideas.

2 LANGUAGE FOCUS: QUANTIFIERS

 Track 17 **A. Listen and practice.**

Do you read *a lot of / many* books?	Yes, I read *a lot* (of books).
	I read *quite a lot.*
	No, I don't read *many.*
	No, I don't read *any.*
Do you watch *a lot of / much* TV?	Yes, I watch *a lot of* TV.
	I watch *quite a lot.*
	No, I don't watch *much* (TV).
	No, I don't watch *any* (TV).

Track 18 **B. Pairs. Complete the conversations with words from the language box in A. Listen and check your answers. Then practice with a partner.**

1. **A:** Do you read _____ books and magazines?

   B: I read quite a _____ of magazines but not many books.

   A: What kinds of magazines?

   B: I read mostly sports and entertainment magazines.

2. **A:** Do you play _____ sports?

   B: _____ a lot. I only play squash on the weekends.

   A: I don't play _____ either. I'm always too busy.

3. **A:** Do you listen to _____ music?

   B: Yeah, I listen to _____ music. I listen to my MP3 all the time.

   A: What kind of music do you listen to?

   B: Mainly country and western. And pop, too.

4. **A:** Do you watch _____ TV?

   B: Yes, I watch it _____ but mainly on the weekends.

   A: What do you like to watch?

   B: I watch a lot of movies and sports programs.

C. Pairs. Practice the conversations again. Use true information.

CD 2 Track 19 **A.** Listen to people talking to friends and number five of the topics they talk about from 1 to 5 in the order you hear about them.

____ a movie   ____ a TV program

____ a concert   ____ a sporting event

____ a book   ____ an opera

B. Listen again. Did the friends like the events? Check (✓) the correct answer.

	They both liked it	One of them liked it	Neither of them liked it
1.			
2.			
3.			
4.			
5.			

4 JOIN IN

A. Pairs. Complete this survey for yourself.

HOW OFTEN DO YOU...	Never	Not very often	Sometimes	Pretty often	WHAT WAS THE LAST ONE YOU...
buy a magazine?	○	○	○	○	bought? _____
read a book?	○	○	○	○	read? _____
read a story on the Internet?	○	○	○	○	read? _____
go to a movie theater?	○	○	○	○	went to? _____
rent a DVD?	○	○	○	○	rented? _____
buy a CD?	○	○	○	○	bought? _____
go to a concert?	○	○	○	○	went to? _____
watch a sports event?	○	○	○	○	watched? _____
watch a late–night movie?	○	○	○	○	watched? _____
watch a documentary on TV?	○	○	○	○	watched? _____
download a song?	○	○	○	○	downloaded? _____

NOW SHOWING!

ONE TICKET   ONE TICKET

B. Pairs. Ask and answer the questions from A. Then talk with a partner about your answers in the last column.

A: *How often do you buy a magazine?*

B: *Not very often. I guess about two or three times a month.*

A: *What was the last one you bought?*

B: _____.

1 THINGS PEOPLE TALK ABOUT

CD 2 Track 20 **A.** Do you ever talk to friends about the things below? Use the key to write your response. Then listen and repeat. What else do you usually talk about?

✓ ✓ = often   ✓ = sometimes   0 = never

1. sports

2. work

3. nightlife

4. music

5. your family

6. vacations

7. hobbies

8. studying

9. shopping

B. Pairs. What topics would you talk about with the people below? Choose from the list above, or add your own ideas. Talk about it with a partner.

People	Topics
a best friend	shopping
a friend's parents	
a classmate	
a foreign visitor	
grandparents	
a teacher	

C. Pairs. Choose one of the topics from A and talk about it with a partner. Use conversation strategies you've learned to keep the conversation going.

A. Pairs. Listen to the conversations. Then practice with a partner.

CD 2 Track 21

1. **A:** *Do you like sports?*
   B: Yes, I enjoy them a lot. Especially tennis.

   A: *Oh, yeah? How long have you been playing tennis?*
   B: For about two years.

2. **A:** *Do you like playing video games?*
   B: Yes, I do. I've got some great games at home.

   A: *And do you spend a lot buying new games?*
   B: Yeah, my parents are always complaining about it.

3. **A:** *Are you interested in music?*
   B: Yes, I am. I'm always downloading stuff from the Internet.

   A: *I see. And do you play any musical instruments?*
   B: Yeah, the trumpet.

B. Notice how small talk is usually about topics of shared interest. We can also use expressions like these to initiate small talk.

Have you seen any good movies lately?
We're having great weather at the moment.
Have you been to any of the summer sales yet?
There are some great programs on TV this week.
Do you watch much football?

Pairs. Now practice the conversations in A again, using different expressions to make small talk.

C. Pairs. You are at a party and you meet the people below. Think of three questions to ask each person. Don't use the same question twice. Then practice asking questions and making up good answers.

A flight attendant	A visitor from Australia	A music student	A retired person

D. Pairs. Practice the conversations in A again. This time use your own information.

LISTEN AND UNDERSTAND

A. Listen to people meeting at a party. What do you think the occupation of each person is? Number the pictures from 1 to 3 in the order you hear about them.

B. Listen again. Check (✓) which of the two statements is true.

1. a. Andrew has never met Mr. Kim before. ☐
    b. Both of the brothers are good at sports. ☐

2. a. Lek made only some of the food at the party. ☐
    b. Lek is still learning her job. ☐

3. a. Simon has already graduated from college. ☐
    b. Simon doesn't know what job he wants in the future. ☐

4 **JOIN IN**

A. Add two topics to the chart. Then write two questions about each topic.

TOPIC	QUESTION 1	QUESTION 2
School or work		
TV		
Movies		
Sports		
Food		
Hobbies		
Your idea: _____		
Your idea: _____		

B. Class activity. Practice asking and answering your questions from A with your classmates. Ask follow-up questions to keep the conversations going.

Talents and Learning

LESSON 1: Talents

1 WHAT ARE YOU GOOD AT?

A. Circle the activities you've had lessons in. What else have you taken lessons in?

1. piano

2. guitar

3. dancing

4. tennis

5. cooking

6. drawing

7. photography

CD 2 Track 23   **B.** Pairs. Listen to the conversation. Then practice with a partner.

A: I have a music lesson today.

B: 1 What instrument do you play?

A: Piano. Can you play the piano?

B: 2 Well, sort of, but I can't play very well. I should take more lessons.

A: Why not? I love the piano.

B: 3 Can you play anything else?

A: Yeah, I'm learning the guitar, too.

C. Pairs. Practice the conversation again. Use this information.

Practice 1

1   Really? What are you learning?

2   Not anymore. I could play when I was a kid.

3   Do you play another instrument?

Practice 2

1   Yeah? What kind of lesson?

2   Yeah. I took some lessons a few years ago.

3   Are you learning anything else?

CD 2 Track 24 **A. Listen and practice.**

Can you play a musical instrument?	Yes, I *can*. I (*can*) play the piano.
	No, I *can't*.
How well *can* she sing?	She *can* sing pretty well.
	She's not too bad.
	She *can't* sing very well.
Could he speak English three years ago?	Yes, he *could*.
	No, he *couldn't*.

CD 2 Track 25 **B. Pairs. Complete the conversations with items from the language box in A. Listen and check your answers. Then practice with a partner.**

1. **A:** _____ you play any musical instruments?
   B: Yeah, I can play the guitar and the drums.
   A: You _____ play the drums! Cool.

2. **A:** How _____ can you sing?
   B: I'm not too bad. I sing with a group at school. How about you?
   A: My friends tell me I have a terrible voice. They say I _____ sing in tune and always miss the right notes.
   B: _____ you sing for me? Let me hear you sing.

3. **A:** Can you play tennis?
   B: Not very well. I _____ play quite well a few years ago, but I haven't played for a while. Do you play?
   A: Yeah, but I _____ play very well. I'm taking lessons at the moment.

4. **A:** _____ you speak English when you were 10?
   B: Yes, I could a little. I started studying English when I was seven. _____ you?
   A: No, I _____. I didn't start to study English until I was 12.

5. **A:** _____ you speak any other foreign languages?
   B: Well, I can speak a little French. I love French.
   A: I _____ speak French but I can speak a little Spanish. I'm taking Spanish 101 this semester.
   B: Let me hear you say a few words in Spanish.
   A: I _____ right now. I'm in a hurry. Maybe later!

C. Pairs. Practice the conversations again. Use true information.

CD 2 Track 26   **A. Listen to Carlo talking about these activities. Can he do these things? Check (✓) the correct column.**

CAN HE...	SING	WATER-SKI	TAKE PHOTOGRAPHS	KAYAK	COOK
Yes, pretty well	☐	☐	☐	☐	☐
Yes, but not very well	☐	☐	☐	☐	☐
No	☐	☐	☐	☐	☐
Learned recently	☐	☐	☐	☐	☐
Learned a long time ago	☐	☐	☐	☐	☐

B. Listen again. When did Carlo learn to do these things? Check (✓) the correct column above.

4   JOIN IN

A. Class activity. Talk to your classmates. Find people who can/could do the things below.

ACTIVITY	NAME
Design a website	_____
Fix computer problems	_____
Ice-skate	_____
Say "good morning" in four languages	_____
Sing a song in a foreign language	_____
Recite a poem in English	_____
Do something better in the past than they can do now	_____
Speak English before they were 10	_____
Read before they started grade school	_____
Drive before they were 16	_____

B. Class activity. Share with the class the two most interesting things you learned in A.

1 THINGS WE LEARN AT COLLEGE

CD 2 Track 27 **A.** Look at the subjects students can study at college in the United States. Check (✓) the ones that sound interesting to you. Then listen and repeat.

1. health education

2. urban planning

3. media studies

4. information and communication technology

5. interior design

6. sales and marketing

7. sociology

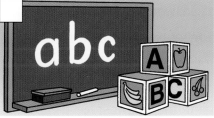

8. childhood education

9. applied arts

B. Look at topics you can learn about when you study the subjects in A. Write the corresponding subject next to each topic. More than one answer is possible.

website design _____

weaving and pottery _____

road design _____

filmmaking _____

citizens' rights _____

nutrition for teenagers _____

how to persuade people _____

choosing colors _____

parks and gardens _____

teenage crime _____

learning to read _____

home decoration _____

C. Pairs. What are your majors? What courses are you studying? Talk with a partner.

2 CONVERSATION STRATEGY: ASKING FOR MORE DETAILS

CD 2 Track 28 **A. Pairs. Listen to the conversations. Then practice with a partner.**

> **1. A:** I really enjoyed the course on information technology.
> **B:** *What did you study in the course?*
> **A:** Well, one of the things we learned was website design.
> **B:** Hey, maybe you can design a website for me!
>
> **2. A:** I took a home ec course recently. It was really useful.
> **B:** *Did the course teach you how to cook?*
> **A:** No, it was all about managing home finances.

B. Notice how we can respond to information by asking for more details. We can also use these expressions:

What did you like about it?

You did? What was the teacher like?

So what was the best thing you learned?

It was? Did you learn how to sew?

Pairs. Now practice the conversations in A again, using different expressions to ask for more details.

C. Pairs. Match the statements to the detail questions. Then practice with a partner and give your own answers to the detail questions.

1. I learned to play the trumpet when I was a teenager.

2. My favorite course at college was on interior design.

3. I'm finding my economics course very difficult.

4. I went to a small college in the Midwest.

5. I speak quite good Spanish. It's a language I like a lot.

____ Do you need to be good at math to do the course?

____ Have you ever been to Spain or Mexico?

____ Do you think it was a good place to go to school?

____ Did the course teach you how to open your own design business?

____ Did you take lessons or did you learn it on your own?

D. Pairs. Practice the conversations in A again. This time add your own detail questions.

CD 2 Track 29

A. **Listen to people talking about their college experiences. What is the topic of the detail questions? Number five of the topics below from 1 to 5 in the order you hear about them.**

____ teachers   ____ courses   ____ cost

____ reasons   ____ examples   ____ location

B. **Listen again. Were the people surprised by the extra detail they heard?**

	Surprised	Not surprised
1.		
2.		
3.		
4.		
5.		

A. **Complete the survey about your high school experience.**

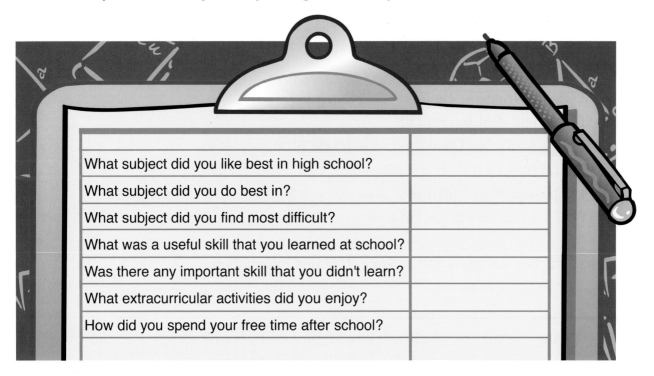

What subject did you like best in high school?	
What subject did you do best in?	
What subject did you find most difficult?	
What was a useful skill that you learned at school?	
Was there any important skill that you didn't learn?	
What extracurricular activities did you enjoy?	
How did you spend your free time after school?	

B. **Pairs. Compare your answers in A with a partner. Ask follow-up questions to get more information.**

A: *What subject did you like best in high school?*

B: *I guess it was chemistry.*

A: *Chemistry! What did you like about it?*

B: *We had a great teacher. He made it really fun and interesting.*

People in the News

LESSON 1: Famous people

1 WHAT DID THEY DO?

A. Pairs. Look at the people in the photos. What were they famous for? Take notes and talk with your partner about what you know.

Walt Disney

Shakespeare

Indira Gandhi

Nureyev

Charlie Chaplin

CD 2 Track 30 **B. Pairs.** Listen to the conversation. Then practice with a partner.

A: What are you reading?

B: 1 A new book by Dan Brown.

A: 2 Oh, he wrote *The Da Vinci Code*, didn't he?

B: That's right. Did you read it?

A: 3 No, I didn't, but I saw the movie. It was great, wasn't it?

B: Yeah, I enjoyed it a lot.

A: 4 What's his new book like?

B: Well, it's really long, but I'm enjoying it so far.

C. Pairs. Practice the conversation again. Use this information.

Practice 1

1 A book by the crime writer P. D. James.

2 Oh, she was the one who wrote *The Murder Room*, wasn't she?

3 No, I didn't, but I saw it on TV. It was really scary, wasn't it?

4 How are you enjoying her new book?

Practice 2

1 A new book by Isabel Allende.

2 Oh, she's great. She wrote *The House of the Spirits*, didn't she?

3 Yes, I did. It was fantastic, wasn't it?

4 What do you think of her new book?

2 LANGUAGE FOCUS: TAG QUESTIONS

A. Listen and practice.

She was a writer, *wasn't she?*	Yes, she was. No, she wasn't.
They were in the Harry Potter movies, *weren't they?*	Yes, they were. No, they weren't.
He wrote *The Da Vinci Code, didn't he?*	Yes, he did. No, he didn't.
They appeared in the *Titanic* movie, *didn't they?*	Yes, they did. No, they didn't

Track 32 **B. Pairs. Complete the conversations with tag questions. Listen and check your answers. Then practice with a partner.**

1. **A:** J. K. Rowling wrote the Harry Potter books, _____?

   B: Yes, she did. I read all of them. They were great, _____?

   A: Yes, they were.

2. **A:** Rain made his first Hollywood film in 2007, _____?

   B: Yes, I think so. And he used to act on television in Korea, _____?

   A: Yes, he did. And of course he was a very successful singer.

3. **A:** Kawabata Yasunari was a very successful writer, _____?

   B: Oh, yes. Very. He wrote *Snow Country* and lots of other novels.

   A: Right. And he won the Nobel Prize for Literature, _____?

   B: Yes. In 1968. I think he was the first Japanese writer to win.

4. **A:** I love Issey Miyake's clothes. He was born in Hiroshima, _____?

   B: The fashion designer, you mean? Yes, he was. That's right.

   A: And he created perfumes too, _____?

   B: Yes. Perfumes and colognes for both women and men.

C. Groups. Write three statements about famous people you know about. Use tag questions. Then share them with the group. What else do your classmates know about these people?

   A: Beyoncé was one of Destiny's Child, wasn't she?

   B: Yes, she was. And so was Michelle Williams.

3 LISTEN AND UNDERSTAND

Track 33 **A.** Listen to conversations about people in the news. Number the people they are talking about from 1 to 5 in the order you hear about them.

____ a writer   ____ an actress

____ an actor   ____ a music group

____ a movie director ____ an opera singer

B. Listen again and circle the correct words.

1. His books *have / haven't been* made into movies.

2. She almost *never / quite often* works in films.

3. They write *most / all* of their own songs.

4. They're *going to see / have already seen* her perform.

5. They *agreed / didn't agree* about his last film.

4 JOIN IN

A. Prepare six statements about famous singers, actors, writers, and movie directors. Make two of your statements false. Then read them to your parnter. Can they correct the false information?

1. _____

2. _____

3. _____

4. _____

5. _____

6. _____

Steven Spielberg directed the movie *Seven Samurai*, didn't he?

No, I don't think so. Kurosawa directed it.

1 SUCCESSFUL PEOPLE IN THE ARTS

CD 2 Track 34 **A.** **Look at the occupations and the people below. Number the pictures with the correct occupation.**

1. an opera singer
2. a composer
3. an actress
4. a novelist
5. a recording artist
6. an artist
7. an illusionist
8. a film director
9. a violinist

Pablo Picasso

David Blaine

Mozart

Yunjin Kim

Peter Jackson

Luciano Pavarotti

Vanessa Mae

Karena Lam

J. K. Rowling

B. Pairs. What have the people in A done? Do you know their work? Talk about it with your partner.

C. Class activity. Can you name five famous people in the arts today from your country or other countries you know? What do they do?

> Sumi Jo is a famous opera singer. She's from Korea.

2 CONVERSATION STRATEGY: EXPRESSING DEGREES OF CERTAINTY

A. Pairs. Listen to the conversations. Then practice with a partner. *Track 35*

1. **A:** Do you know when the Beatles first became popular?

   B: *I'm pretty sure it was in the 1960s.*

   A: Are you sure? Wasn't it later than that?

   B: *It could have been in the 1970s.* Somewhere around then, I think.

2. **A:** Do you remember who wrote the James Bond novels?

   B: *I'm not sure, but I'm almost certain it was Ian Fleming.*

   A: And when did he write them?

   B: *I'm not sure. I suppose it was in the 1950s or 60s.*

B. Notice how we can express degrees of certainty. We can also use these expressions:

When did the Beatles first become popular?

It must have been...   *more certain*

I'm almost certain it was...

I'm pretty sure it was...

It was most likely...

It could have been...

I suppose it was...   *less certain*

Pairs. Now practice the conversations in A again, using different expressions to show degrees of certainty.

C. Pairs. Practice asking and answering these questions. Choose expressions to express how certain you are of the answer.

1. **A.** Who recorded the song *We Belong Together*?

   B: _____ (Madonna, Mariah Carey, CoCo Lee)

2. **A.** Who wrote the opera *Madam Butterfly*?

   B: _____ (Puccini, Mozart, Elton John)

3. **A.** Who wrote the song *Imagine*?

   B: _____ (Elvis Presley, Stevie Wonder, John Lennon)

4. **A.** When did the first Harry Potter movie come out?

   B: _____ (1999, 2001, 2003)

D. Pairs. Practice the conversations in A again. This time use your own information.

Track 36 **A.** Listen to information about people in the arts. Add the missing information.

Internet Search

Address http://www.fansofkarena.fans

Karena Lam

Born

Vancouver, _____, 1978

First album

1999

Family

Father from Hong Kong,

_____

Half Japanese, half Chinese

from _____

Based in

Taiwan

Trivia

♥ Was working in her family's shop when she was discovered

♥ Has appeared in commercials for _____

Get Karena Lam ringtones here!

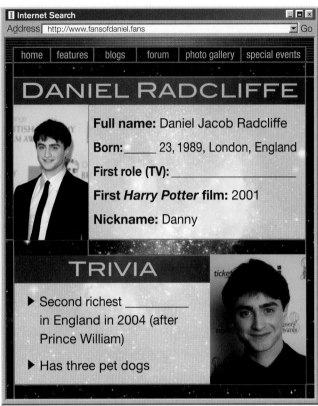

Internet Search

Address http://www.fansofdaniel.fans

home | features | blogs | forum | photo gallery | special events

DANIEL RADCLIFFE

Full name: Daniel Jacob Radcliffe

Born: _____ 23, 1989, London, England

First role (TV): _____

First *Harry Potter* film: 2001

Nickname: Danny

TRIVIA

▶ Second richest _____ in England in 2004 (after Prince William)

▶ Has three pet dogs

B. Listen again and correct any errors in the information you wrote.

A. Pairs. Work together to prepare four questions like this about famous people.

Who was the musical Phantom of the Opera *written by? Was it Elton John or Andrew Lloyd Webber?*

When did Picasso live? Was it in the 19th century or the 20th century?

B. Group activity. Take turns asking and answering your questions from A.

unit
12 Shopping

LESSON 1: In a store

1 WHERE CAN I FIND CHILDREN'S TOYS?

A. Circle the items you have bought recently. What else have you bought?

1. shoes   **2.** CD   **3.** T-shirt   **4.** book   **5.** magazine   **6.** chocolates   **7.** baseball cap

 Track 37 **B. Pairs. Listen to the conversation. Then practice with a partner.**

A: Can I help you?

B: Yes. I'm looking for a gift for a six-year-old. **1** Can you tell me where I can find toys and things for kids?

A: Sure, that would be on the second floor, near the elevator.

B: Thanks. **2** And do you sell sandwiches or cakes here?

A: No, I'm afraid not. There are no restaurants or other places to eat in the store.

B: OK. **3** Well, do you know where I can get something light to eat around here?

A: Actually, there's a very nice cafe about a block down the street. It's called Superchef. It's great.

B: **4** Thanks very much. I'll try it.

C. Pairs. Practice the conversation again. Use this information.

Practice 1

1 Do you know where the children's section is?

2 Could you tell me if there's a cafeteria in the store?

3 Do you know if there's a cafe or something near here?

4 It sounds perfect. Thanks.

Practice 2

1 Do you know if there's a toy section here?

2 Is there anywhere to buy food in the store?

3 Can you tell me where I could get something to eat?

4 That'll do. Thanks a lot.

CD 2 Track 38 **A.** Listen and practice.

	Embedded *yes/no* questions
Is there a cafe near here?	Do you know *if there's a cafe near here?*
	Could you tell me *if there's a cafe near here?*
	Embedded *Wh-* questions
Where can I buy toys?	Can you tell me *where I can buy toys?*
Where's the closest ATM?	Do you know *where the closest ATM is?*
When does the store close?	Do you know *when the store closes?*
	Could you tell me *when the store closes?*

CD 2 Track 39 **B.** Pairs. Rewrite the questions below as embedded questions. Listen and check your answers. Then practice with a partner. (Answers may vary.)

1. **A:** _____?
   [What hours are department stores open here?]
   B: Yeah, I think they usually open at 10 in the morning and close at 6 p.m.

2. **A:** _____?
   [Is there a good store in this neighborhood?]
   B: Yes, I think Liberty House is pretty good.

3. **A:** _____?
   [Are they having any sales at the moment?]
   B: I'm not sure. But if you like, we can look in the paper to check.

4. **A:** Good idea. _____? [And where's a good place to get computers and electronic stuff?]
   B: Computer World on High Street is pretty good. They have a good selection and their prices are reasonable.

5. **A:** A couple more things. _____?
   [Where's a good place to buy clothes?]
   B: I always find they have good things at the stores on Pine Street.

6. **A:** OK. _____? [And do all of the stores there take credit cards?]
   B: I don't know for sure, but I think they do.

C. Pairs. Practice the conversations again. Use true information.

3 LISTEN AND UNDERSTAND

CD 2 Track 40 **A.** Listen to people in different sections of a store. Number where they are from 1 to 5 in the order you hear about them.

B. Listen again. Check (✓) which of the two statements is true.

1. **a.** He likes cotton. ____
   b. He bought them without trying them on. ____

2. **a.** He's looking for a table and chairs. ____
   b. He decided to take the first set. ____

3. **a.** The radio has a manual. ____
   b. They weren't able to tune into a Spanish station. ____

4. **a.** He is in the sporting goods department. ____
   b. He wants to play ice-hockey. ____

5. **a.** He asked how long they would take to develop. ____
   b. She advised him not to smile. ____

4 JOIN IN

A. Groups. Where is a good place to buy these things in your town or city? Complete the form, then discuss with your group members.

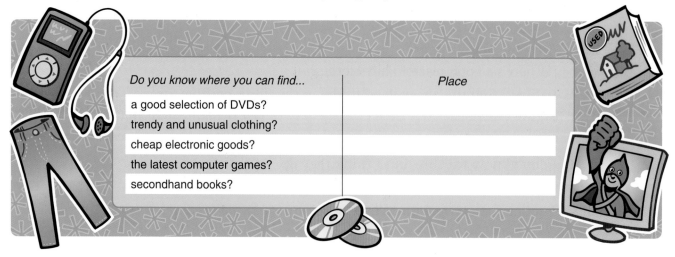

Do you know where you can find...	Place
a good selection of DVDs?	
trendy and unusual clothing?	
cheap electronic goods?	
the latest computer games?	
secondhand books?	

A: Do you know where you can find a good selection of DVDs?

B: Maybe at Studio Records. You can also get cheap DVDs at...

1 PROBLEMS WITH PURCHASES

  Track 41 **A. Match the problems with the items. Then listen and repeat.**

1. a tear   3. a crack   5. damaged   7. a stain   9. a scratch

2. a hole   4. broken   6. something missing   8. a burn mark

B. Pairs. Look at the things that people have purchased. How many problems can you find? Compare what you've found with your partner.

A: The table has a missing leg.

B: The leg of the table has a crack.

C. Pairs. Look around the classroom. Can you find items in the classroom with any of the problems from A? Discuss what you find with your partner.

A. Pairs. Listen to the conversations. Then practice with a partner.

1. **A:** I'm sorry, there's a problem with this shirt.

   B: Really? What's the problem?

   A: *There seems to be a stain on it, right here.*

   B: Yes, I see what you mean. Let me get you a new one.

2. **A:** I think there's something wrong with this CD player.

   B: Really? What seems to be the problem?

   A: *I don't think it's working like it should.*

   B: Let me check it for you.

B. Notice how we can make complaints politely by being vague. We can also use these expressions:

I think there might be a…
Well, I just happened to notice…
It seems like it just isn't working…

Pairs. Now practice the conversations in A again, using different expressions to make polite complaints.

C. Pairs. Choose phrases to complete these conversations. Then practice with a partner.

> *It doesn't seem to be working right.*   *Yes, it seems to have a tear in the collar.*
> *Well, the heel seems to be damaged.*   *It looks like it has a crack in it.*

1. **A:** Excuse me, but there's a problem with this watch.

   B: Really? What seems to be wrong with it?

   A: _____

   B: I'll take a look at it for you.

2. **A:** There's something wrong with this shirt.

   B: There is?

   A: _____

   B: Yes, it does. Let me get another one for you.

3. **A:** Is that shoe OK?

   B: _____

   A: Really? Let me get another one for you.

D. Pairs. Practice the conversations again. This time suggest a different problem with each item.

 Track 43 **A.** Listen to people describing problems with things they've bought. Number five of the items from 1 to 5 in the order you hear about them.

B. Listen again. What happened in each case? Choose the correct answer.

    a. The item was exchanged for another.
    b. The store gave a refund.
    c. The customer kept the item.

1. ____   **2.** ____   **3.** ____   **4.** ____   **5.** ____

4 JOIN IN

A. Role-play. Take turns being a store clerk and a customer who is returning things to a store. First write about problems with the items below, then practice conversations like the one below.

MP3 player

laptop computer

DVD

shirt

watch

Clerk: Can I help you?

Customer: Yes, I bought this clock the other day, but there seems to be a problem with it.

Clerk: Really? What appears to be the problem?

Customer: Well, there seems to be something broken at the back.

Clerk: Let me take a look. Yes, I see what you mean. Let me get you another one. Do you have your receipt, by the way?

Customer: Yes, here it is.

Clerk: Thanks. Sorry about the problem. I'll just be a minute.

4 JOIN IN

A. **Role-play. Take turns being a patient and a doctor at a health clinic. Use the sample dialogue and problems below. Student B looks at this page. Student A looks at page 17.**

A: *What can I do for you today?*

B: *I have _____.*

A: *That's too bad. How long have you had the problem?*

B: *For a week.*

A: *Mmm. I see. Well, I'll give you _____.*

B: *Thank you very much.*

Problem	How long?	Treatment
the flu	four days	rest and something for your throat
a fever	two days	some tablets and something to help you sleep

Review

QUESTIONS WITH *LIKE / INTERESTED IN*; OBJECT PRONOUNS

A. Review the language box.

Do you like film music?	Yes, I really like *it*.
Does he like Jane?	Yes, he likes *her*.
Does she like Bob?	Yes, she likes *him*.
Do you like action movies?	Yeah, I like *them* a lot.
	Yes, I love *them*.
	They're OK.
	No, I don't like *them* very much.
	No, I can't stand *them*.
Are you interested in pop music?	Yes, I am. I like *it* a lot.
	No, I'm not very interested in *it*.
Are you interested in old movies?	No, I don't like *them* at all.

B. Complete the conversations. Use language from Unit 1.

1. **A:** Do you _____ action movies?

   B: Yes, I do. What about you?

   A: Yeah, I like _____ a lot. I'm crazy about Jet Li—his movies are great.

   B: Oh, I haven't seen _____.

2. **A:** Do you _____ the Harry Potter movies?

   B: Yes, I do. Why?

   A: Well, there's a Harry Potter film festival next week. Are you _____ in going?

   B: Sure! That sounds great.

3. **A:** Do you _____ baseball?

   B: Oh, _____ OK. What about you?

   A: Um, I really like _____.

4. **A:** Are you _____ in jazz music?

   B: I don't know. I don't know much about _____. How about you?

   A: Yes, I really like _____.

5. **A:** Do you _____ to watch science fiction movies?

   B: Oh, yes. They're my favorites. Especially the Matrix movies.

   A: Me too. I've seen two of _____. The special effects are really cool.

UNIT 2

PRESENT PERFECT TENSE AND PAST TENSE

A. Review the language box.

Have you ever broken your arm?	Yes, *I have.*
	No, *I haven't.*
	Yes, *I broke* my arm a few years ago.
Has he ever been in the hospital?	Yes, *he has.* / No, *he hasn't.*
she	Yes, *she has.* / No, *she hasn't.*
they	Yes, *they have.* / No, *they haven't.*
I've twisted	my ankle a couple of times.
He's also *twisted*	his ankle.
She's never *twisted*	her ankle.
I *twisted*	my ankle last summer.

B. Complete the conversations. Use language from Unit 2.

1. **A:** _____ you ever _____ (*play*) baseball?

   B: Yes, I _____ (*have*). I _____ (*play*) a lot—I'm on the school team.

2. **A:** What _____ (*happen*) to Tom?

   B: He _____ (*burn*) his hand.

   A: How did he do that?

   B: Oh, he was cooking and the oil _____ (*be*) too hot.

   A: Oh, that's terrible. I hope it's not too serious.

3. **A:** I don't feel well. I have a really sore throat.

   B: Oh, that's too bad. _____ you _____ (*take*) anything for it?

   A: No, not yet.

   B: Well, you should get some throat spray from the drugstore.

4. **A:** So, how are you today?

   B: Not very well. I have a backache.

   A: I see. How long _____ you _____ (*have*) the problem?

   B: For a week.

5. **A:** Have you _____ (*go*) hiking?

   B: Yes, I _____ (*go*) last year. How about you?

   B: Oh, yes. I _____ (*go*) many times.

UNIT 3

COMPARATIVES

A. Review the language box.

Which one do you like *better*?	I like this one *better.*
Which one is *more expensive*?	This one is *more expensive.*
Which ones are *cheaper*?	These are *cheaper.*
Which one costs *more*?	This one costs *more.*
Do you think this one is *good*?	No, I like this one *better.*
Silk is *more expensive than* cotton.	
It's *more comfortable.*	
Silk is *lighter than* cotton.	
Cotton is *easier* to wash.	
Note: use *more* with *comfortable, expensive.*	

B. Complete the conversations. Use language from Unit 3.

1. **A:** What do you think? Should I buy the dark shirt or the light shirt?

   B: The light one, I think. I think it suits you _____ (*good*).

   A: I do too.

2. **A:** Is Yuriko a _____ (*good*) tennis player than I am?

   B: I'm not sure. She hits the ball _____ (*hard*) than you, but you
   move _____ (*fast*).

3. **A:** So, how is college compared to high school?

   B: Well, it's _____ (*difficult*) than high school.

4. **A:** Which jacket are you going to buy Jae-won?

   B: This one. It's _____ (*expensive*) than the other one, but the cloth is better.

5. **A:** These sweaters are cute. Which do you like _____ (*good*)?

   B: They're both cute, but I think I like the pink one _____ (*good*).
   It's _____ (*stylish*).

   A: I agree. And it feels _____ (*soft*) too.

UNIT 4

SUPERLATIVES

A. Review the language box.

What's *the nearest* subway stop?	It's on Main Street.
Where's *the best* supermarket?	It's near the subway.
What's *the closest* park?	It's Brookdale, just around the corner.
What's *the busiest* street?	Main is *the busiest*.
Where are *the most interesting* shops?	In the mall.
Where are *the tallest* buildings?	Downtown.
Where is *the worst* traffic?	In the city center.
Note: use *the most* with *beautiful, famous, interesting, expensive, popular.*	

B. Complete the conversations. Use language from Unit 4.

1. **A:** What's _____ (*interesting*) city you've been to?

   B: Oh, Montreal—I think it's _____ (*pretty*) city in Canada.

2. **A:** What's _____ (*good*) street for cafes?

   B: Oh, that's Ninth Avenue. It's a really cool area.

3. **A:** What's _____ (*easy*) way to get to the airport?

   B: The airport bus is _____ (*convenient*) and it's also _____ (*cheap*)—a taxi costs a lot more.

4. **A:** Who's _____ (*good*) teacher at this school?

   B: Well, I think Ms. Santiago is _____ (*good*).

5. **A:** Who's _____ (*rich*) person in the world?

   B: Well, some people say Bill Gates is _____ (*rich*).

6. **A:** What country has _____ (*big*) population?

   B: I think China does.

7. **A:** What's _____ (*tall*) tower in the world?

   B: Is it the CN Tower in Canada?

   B: Yes, I think it is.

8. **A:** What's _____ (*bad*) thing in your neighborhood?

   B: My neighbors! They are _____ (*noisy*) people I know.

UNIT 5

SIMPLE PAST QUESTIONS

A. Review the language box.

Did you *have* a good weekend?	Yes, I did.
Did you *go* to a movie on Saturday night?	No, I didn't. I stayed home.
What *did* you *do* on Sunday?	I saw a movie.
Where *did* you *go*?	I went to a party.
Who *did* you *go* with?	I went with a few friends.
How *was* your weekend?	It was great.
What *did* he *do* yesterday?	He studied for a test.
Where *did* she *go* Saturday?	She went out with friends.
Where *did* they *go* on vacation?	They went to Florida.

B. Complete the conversations. Use language from Unit 5.

1. **A:** _____ you _____ (*enjoy*) your vacation?

    B: Yes, it _____ (*be*) terrific, thanks.

    A: Where _____ you _____ (*go*)?

    B: We went to Hawaii. It's gorgeous!

2. **A:** _____ you _____ (*go*) to the basketball game last night?

    B: Yes, I did. It _____ (*be*) great. What did you and Maria do last night?

    A: We _____ tired, so we _____ (*stay*) home and _____ (*watch*) TV.

3. **A:** _____ you _____ (*go*) anywhere last weekend?

    B: Yeah, I _____ (*go*) to the beach on Saturday.

    A: Oh, yeah? _____ you _____ (*go*) surfing?

    B: No, the waves weren't good, so I _____ (*swim*) instead.

4. **A:** _____ you _____ (*study*) over the weekend?

    B: No, I didn't. _____ (*do*) you?

    A: Yes, I _____ (*study*) a little bit.

5. **A:** _____ your parents _____ (*buy*) a new car?

    B: No. Why do you ask?

    A: I _____ (*see*) a sports car in front of your house.

    B: Oh, that's my uncle's car.

UNIT 6

VERBS OF OBLIGATION

A. Review the language box.

What do I *have to* take?	You *don't have to* take anything.
What *does* he *have to* take?	He *has to* take a gift.
Do we *have to* take anything?	You *could* take some flowers.
Does she *need to* take something?	She *ought to* take something.
What *should* they take?	They *should* take a small gift.
You *shouldn't* arrive late.	
You *need to* arrive on time.	
Note: *could, should,* and *ought to* are followed by the base form of the verb.	

B. Complete the conversations. Use language from Unit 6.

1. **A:** I've been invited to a barbecue at my manager's house. What kind of clothes
   _____ I wear?

   B: Well, you _____ wear anything too formal. You should wear
   something casual.

   A: OK. And what time _____ I arrive? Is it OK to arrive early?

   B: No, you _____ arrive early. It's all right to arrive a little late, but you _____
   arrive too late. You _____ to be there about 15 to 30 minutes after the time
   your host has said.

2. **A:** Have you ever been to a baby shower before?

   B: Yes, I have. Why?

   A: I've been invited to one for someone from work, but I don't know
   what to bring.

   B: Well, you _____ buy a gift—for the baby.

   A: Really? Do I _____ to buy something expensive?

   B: No, you don't _____ to. You can buy a small present.

UNIT 7

PAST TENSE AND PAST CONTINUOUS

A. Review the language box.

I *ran* into a wall	while I *was parking* the car.
I *damaged* the car	while I *was taking* it out of the garage.
I *bumped* into another car	while I *was passing* it.
You *dropped* a dish	while you *were cooking*.
He *called*	while you *were watching* TV.
She *lost* her wallet	while she *was traveling* in Europe.
They *saw* the accident	while they *were walking* to work.
We *fell* asleep	while we *were watching* a movie.

B. Complete the conversations. Use language from Unit 7.

1. **A:** Where's your camera?

   B: I _____ (*take*) a picture at the river, and I _____ (*drop*) it in the water.

   A: Oh, no. It was a really nice one too.

2. **A:** What happened to your hand?

   B: I _____ (*chop*) vegetables and _____ (*cut*) my finger.

   A: Oh, no. Does it hurt?

   B: Well, it did. But it's not too bad now.

3. **A:** I _____ (*see*) Ken yesterday.

   B: Really? Where did you see him?

   A: Denise and I _____ (*eat*) lunch at a cafe, and he _____ (*come*) in.

   B: Oh, and _____ (*talk*) to him?

   A: Yes, he _____ (*sit*) down and we had a nice time.

4. **A:** So, how did you two meet?

   B: I _____ (*work*) in London when we _____ (*meet*).

   A: Really? What were you doing there?

   B: I _____ (*work*) in a bank and she _____ (*be*) my boss.

UNIT 8

GOING TO AND *WILL* FOR FUTURE

A. Review the language box.

What *are* you *going to* do for summer vacation?	I *'m going to* go to Indonesia.
What *will* you *do* for summer vacation?	I *'ll* probably *go to* Indonesia.
What *'s* he *going to* do for summer vacation?	He's *going to* go to Indonesia.
Are you *going to* travel with friends?	Yes, I *am*.
Will you travel with friends?	Yes, I *will*. / No, I *won't*.
	No, I *'m* not *going to*.
Is she *going to* travel this summer?	Yes, she *is*. / No, she *isn't*.
Are they *going* to visit friends?	Yes, they *are*. / No, they *'re not*.

B. Complete the conversations. Use language from Unit 8.

1. **A:** What are you _____ do next summer?

   B: I'm _____ go to Blue Lake for a couple of weeks.

   A: Oh, yeah? That sounds nice.

2. **A:** Are you _____ go back home next summer?

   B: Yes, I think I _____. I really miss my family.

3. **A:** What are you _____ do after you graduate?

   B: I'm going _____ go to Green Island.

   A: Yeah? What are you _____ do there?

   B: Well, first I _____ travel around for a while. But I _____ also look for work there.

   A: How long _____ you stay there?

   B: I'll be there for eight weeks altogether.

4. **A:** Hi, Mom. I'm _____ study with Josh after class today.

   B: OK. _____ you be home for dinner?

   A: I don't know. I _____ call you.

   B: Well, all right.

5. **A:** What are you _____ do this weekend?

   B: I'm _____ go to the movies with a friend. Do you want to come?

   A: Sure. That sounds great. Thanks.

UNIT 9

QUANTIFIERS

A. Review the language box.

Do you read *a lot of / many* books?	Yes, I read *a lot* (of books).
	I read *quite a lot*.
	No, I don't read *many*.
	No, I don't read *any*.
Do you watch *a lot of / much* TV?	Yes, I watch *a lot of* TV.
	I watch *quite a lot*.
	No, I don't watch *much* (TV).
	No, I don't watch *any* (TV).
Note: we don't have to repeat the noun in response to a question with a quantifier.	

B. Complete the conversations. Use language from Unit 9.

1. **A:** Are you going to the concert this weekend?

   B: No, I'm not. I don't go to _____ concerts because the tickets are so expensive.

2. **A:** Are there _____ students at your school?

   B: Yes, it's a big school, so there are _____ of students.

3. **A:** Do you go to _____ football games?

   B: Yes, my friends are on the team, so I go to _____.

4. **A:** Do you like cooking?

   B: Yes, I like it _____. In fact, I'm a chef!

5. **A:** Do you like playing video games?

   B: Oh, yeah. I like them _____.

   A: Do you spend _____ time playing?

   B: Yes. And my parents complain about it _____!

6. **A:** What kinds of programs do you like to watch?

   B: I watch _____ of movies and sports programs.

UNIT 10

MODAL VERB *CAN* (FOR ABILITY)

A. Review the language box.

Can you play a musical instrument?	Yes, I *can*. I (*can*) play the piano.
	No, I *can't*.
How well *can* she sing?	She *can* sing pretty well.
	Not too bad.
	She *can't* sing very well.
Could he speak English three years ago?	Yes, he *could*.
	No, he *couldn't*.
Can they draw?	Yes, they *can*.
	No, they *can't*.

B. Complete the conversations. Use language from Unit 10.

1. **A:** Dad, when you were nine, _____ you play the piano?

   B: Yes, I _____. I played every day.

   A: Really? Why don't you play now?

2. **A:** My mom is a terrific cook. She _____ make all kinds of food.

   B: Oh, yeah? And what about you? _____ you cook?

   A: No, I _____! I burn everything.

3. **A:** _____ you water-ski, Carlo?

   B: Not very well. What about you?

   A: I don't know. I've never tried water-skiing.

4. **A:** Do you know anyone who _____ design websites?

   B: Yes, my sister _____. She's very creative.

   A: Well, do you think she _____ design one for me?

5. **A:** _____ you speak English better now than you _____ when you started this course?

   B: Yes, I think I _____.

UNIT 11

TAG QUESTIONS

A. Review the language box.

You're in my English class, *aren't you*?	Yes, I am.
	No, I'm not.
She was a writer, *wasn't she*?	Yes, she was.
	No, she wasn't.
He wrote *The Da Vinci Code*, *didn't he*?	Yes, he did.
	No, he didn't.
We have a test tomorrow, *don't we*?	Yes, we do.
	No, we don't.
They were in the Harry Potter movies, *weren't they*?	Yes, they were.
	No, they weren't.
They appeared in the *Titanic* movie, *didn't they*?	Yes, they did.
	No, they didn't

B. Complete the conversations. Use language from Unit 11.

1. **A:** Hi, I think we've met before, _____?

   B: I'm not sure. Do you go to City University?

   A: Yes, I do.

2. **A:** Jim Carrey always makes comedies, _____?

   B: Well, he usually does, but he has also made a drama.

   A: Oh, yes, that's right.

3. **A:** I love action movies, and I really like Jet Li's movies.

   B: Jet Li? He's from the U.S., _____?

   A: No, I think he was born in Beijing.

4. **A:** You can play the piano, _____?

   B: Yes, but I don't play very well.

5. **A:** *Titanic* was based on a true story, _____?

   B: Yes. Definitely. It happened in 1912.

   A: It was a great film, _____? Who was the star?

   B: Um. I think it was Leonardo di Caprio, _____?

UNIT 12

EMBEDDED QUESTIONS

A. Review the language box.

	Embedded *Yes/No* questions
Is there a cafe near here?	Do you know *if there's a cafe near here?*
	Could you tell me *if there's a cafe near here?*
Are there any shoe stores around here?	Do you know *if there are any shoe stores around here?*
	Could you tell me *if there are any shoe stores around here?*
	Embedded *Wh-* questions
Where can I buy toys?	Can you tell me *where I can buy toys?*
Where's the closest ATM?	Do you know *where the closest ATM is?*
When does the store close?	Do you know *when the store closes?*
	Could you tell me *when the store closes?*
What's the nearest subway station?	Do you know *what the nearest subway station is?*

B. Complete the conversations. Use language from Unit 12.

1. **A:** _____? [Does this shirt come in a different color?]

   B: No, I'm sorry. We only have it in blue.

2. **A:** _____? [Is there an ATM near here?]

   B: Yes, there's one in the convenience store next door.

3. **A:** Oh, no! There's a stain on my pants. _____?
   [Where's the nearest dry cleaner's?]

   B: I'm not sure. But if you like, I'll look online to find out.

4. **A:** Do you have everything you need for vacation?

   B: Almost. I just want to buy a book for the plane ride.
   _____? [Where's a good bookstore around here?]

5. **A:** Welcome to the National Museum. How may I help you?

   B: _____? [Where is the Egyptian art?]

   A: It's on the second floor.

   B: Thank you very much.

Vocabulary

UNIT 1

action

animated

art exhibition

baseball game

be interested in

car show

comedy

dance competition

drama

film festival

go out

horror

ice-skating competition

it

movies

musical

play (*n*)

rock concert

romance

science fiction

sorry

tae kwan do demonstration

talent show

them

western

UNIT 2

acupuncture

ankle

antacid tablets

antiseptic cream

arm

aspirin

bandages

bee

brace

break (*v*)

cast

cold (*n*)

cough drops

cut (*n*)

dry skin

eye drops

faint (*v*)

fall

fever

headache

indigestion

infection

lotion

muscle ointment

muscle pain

scratch (*n*)

sling

sore eye

sore throat

sting

throat spray

twist (*v*)

UNIT 3

attractive

belt

better

boots

boring

bracelet

cheaper

cool

earrings

jacket

jeans

more expensive

necklace

old-fashioned

pants

sandals

scarf

shirt

shoes

shorts

sneakers

socks

stylish

sunglasses

sweater

tie

top

umbrella

wallet

watch

UNIT 4

apologize

best

cleanliness

complain

convenience

convenience store

costs

drugstore

elevator

most

neighborhood

newsstand

noise level

parking

public transportation

recreational facility

rent

safety

security

services

supermarket

UNIT 5

beach

car race

catch a wave

dog show

eat out

entry fee

events

farmer's market

food fair

go to a party

gym

I'm not sure.

international

mountains

movie theater

next

sleep in

stay home

street festival

video game

visit friends

weekend

world music festival

UNIT 6

anniversary

baby shower

birthday cake

bring

candy

card

confetti

could

decorations

exchange

firecrackers

flowers

gift

light (v)

ought

picnic

put up

send

should

shouldn't

sing

So that means…

take off

thank-you note

throw

traditional songs

UNIT 7

accident

airline

appointment

best friend

borrow

damage

ever

forget

get into trouble

get lost

ID

lose

miss (v)

mistake

pay attention

rob

trip (v)

What happened?

UNIT 8

bellhop

by myself

camping trip

car trip

chef

driver

flight

foreign

guest

hotel

kitchen assistant

long

office

receptionist

room attendant

security guard

server

summer

telephone operator

uniform

vacation

UNIT 9

a lot (of)

book (*n*)

concert

documentary

download

evening

family

hobbies

lately

listen

mainly

music

nature program

nightlife

opera

reading

sporting event

sports

studying

TV program

visitor

work

UNIT 10

piano

guitar

sort of

well (*adv*)

dancing

tennis

cooking

drawing

photography

kayak

health education

urban planning

media studies

information technology

interior design

sales and marketing

sociology

child education

applied arts

website design

how to persuade people

weaving and pottery

choosing colors

road design

parks and gardens

filmmaking

teenage crime

citizens' rights

learning to read

nutrition for teenagers

home decoration

cost

reasons

examples

location

UNIT 11

actor

actress

almost

artist

ballet dancer

certain

composer

film director

illusionist

most likely

movie director

music group

novelist

opera singer

pretty sure

recording artist

violinist

writer

UNIT 12

toy

CD

T-shirt

Do you know…?

magazine

chocolates

baseball cap

photography

electronics

children's

furniture

sporting goods

menswear

tear (*n*)

hole

crack (*n*)

broken

damaged

something missing

stain (*n*)

burn mark

seem to be

Student CD Track List

This CD contains highlights from each unit
plus new conversations for extra practice.

Unit	Track	Content
	1	Title and copyright
1	2	Page 6, Activity B
	3	Page 6, Activity C, Practice 1
	4	Page 6, Activity C, Practice 2
2	5	Page 12, Activity B
	6	Page 12, Activity C, Practice 1
	7	Page 12, Activity C, Practice 2
3	8	Page 18, Activity B
	9	Page 18, Activity C, Practice 1
	10	Page 18, Activity C, Practice 2
4	11	Page 24, Activity B
	12	Page 24, Activity C, Practice 1
	13	Page 24, Activity C, Practice 2
5	14	Page 30, Activity B
	15	Page 30, Activity C, Practice 1
	16	Page 30, Activity C, Practice 2
6	17	Page 36, Activity B
	18	Page 36, Activity C, Practice 1
	19	Page 36, Activity C, Practice 2

Unit	Track	Content
7	20	Page 42, Activity B
	21	Page 42, Activity C, Practice 1
	22	Page 42, Activity C, Practice 2
8	23	Page 48, Activity B
	24	Page 48, Activity C, Practice 1
	25	Page 48, Activity C, Practice 2
9	26	Page 54, Activity B
	27	Page 54, Activity C, Practice 1
	28	Page 54, Activity C, Practice 2
10	29	Page 60, Activity B
	30	Page 60, Activity C, Practice 1
	31	Page 60, Activity C, Practice 2
11	32	Page 66, Activity B
	33	Page 66, Activity C, Practice 1
	34	Page 66, Activity C, Practice 2
12	35	Page 72, Activity B
	36	Page 72, Activity C, Practice 1
	37	Page 72, Activity C, Practice 2

A separate Class Audio CD containing the complete
audio program is available for teachers.